Holt Geometry

Lesson Plans

HOLT, RINEHART AND WINSTON

A Harcourt Education Company

Orlando • **Austin** • New York • San Diego • London

Printed in the United States of America
ISBN 0-03-078094-2

1 2 3 4 5 6 7 8 9 862 09 08 07 06

Contents

Holt Geometry

Teacher's Name _____ Class _____ Date _____

Lesson Plan 1-1
Understanding Points, Lines, and Planes pp. 6–11   Day _____

Objectives Identify, name, and draw points, lines, segments, rays, and planes. Apply basic facts about points, lines, and planes.

NCTM Standards: students should understand meanings of operations and how they relate to one another.

Pacing
☐ 45-minute Classes: 1 day   ☐ 90-minute Classes: 1/2 day   ☐ Other_____

WARM UP
☐ Warm Up TE p. 6 and Warm Up Transparency 1-1
☐ Countdown to Testing Transparency, Week 1

TEACH
☐ Lesson Presentation CD-ROM 1-1
☐ Alternate Opener, Exploration Transparency 1-1, TE p. 6
☐ Reaching All Learners TE p. 6
☐ Additional Examples Transparencies 1-1
☐ Teaching Transparency 1-1
☐ *Know-It Notebook* 1-1

PRACTICE AND APPLY
☐ Examples 1-2: Basic: 13–17, 33 Average: 13–17, 33, 36, 43 Advanced: 13–17, 33, 34, 36, 43–45
☐ Examples 1-4: Basic: 13–28, 31–33, 39–42, 47–51 Average: 13–28, 30–33, 35–43, 46–51 Advanced: 14–28 even, 29–51

REACHING ALL LEARNERS – Differentiated Instruction for students with

Developing Knowledge	On-level Knowledge	Advanced Knowledge	English Language Development
☐ Modeling TE p. 6	☐ Modeling TE p. 6	☐ Modeling TE p. 6	☐ Modeling TE p. 6
☐ Practice A 1-1 CRB	☐ Practice B 1-1 CRB	☐ Practice C 1-1 CRB	☐ Practice A, B, or C 1-1 CRB
☐ Reteach 1-1 CRB		☐ Challenge 1-1 CRB	☐ *Success for ELL* 1-1
☐ Homework Help Online Keyword: MR4 1-1	☐ Homework Help Online Keyword: MR4 1-1	☐ Homework Help Online Keyword: MR4 1-1	☐ Homework Help Online Keyword: MR4 1-1
☐ *Lesson Tutorial Video* 1-1	☐ *Lesson Tutorial Video* 1-1	☐ *Lesson Tutorial Video* 1-1	☐ *Lesson Tutorial Video* 1-1
☐ Reading *Strategies* 1-1 CRB	☐ Problem Solving 1-1 CRB	☐ Problem Solving 1-1 CRB	☐ Reading *Strategies* 1-1 CRB
☐ Questioning Strategies TE p. 6, 7	☐ Communicating Math TE p. 9	☐ Algebra TE p. 11	☐ Vocabulary Exercises SE p.6
☐ *IDEA Works!* 1-1			☐ *Multilingual Glossary*

ASSESSMENT
☐ Lesson Quiz, TE p. 11 and Transparency 1-1
☐ State-Specific Test Prep Online Keyword: MR4 TestPrep

Holt Geometry

Lesson Plan 1-2
Measuring and Constructing Segments pp. 13-19 Day _____

Objectives Use length and midpoint of a segment. Construct midpoints and congruent segments.

NCTM Standards: students should understand patterns, relations, and functions.

Pacing
☐ 45-minute Classes: 1 day   ☐ 90-minute Classes: 1/2 day   ☐ Other_____

WARM UP
☐ Warm Up TE p. 13 and Warm Up Transparency 1-2
☐ Countdown to Testing Transparency, Week 1

TEACH
☐ Lesson Presentation CD-ROM 12-2
☐ Alternate Opener, Exploration Transparency 1-2, TE p. 13
☐ Reaching All Learners TE p. 14
☐ Additional Examples Transparencies 1-2
☐ Teaching Transparency 1-2
☐ *Geometry Lab Activities* 1-2
☐ *Know-It Notebook* 1-2

PRACTICE AND APPLY
☐ Examples 1-3: Basic: 11–15, 20, 24, 26 Average: 11–15, 20, 24, 26, 28–30, 35, 36, 43 Advanced: 11–15, 20, 24, 26, 28–30, 35, 36, 42–45
☐ Examples 1-5: Basic: 11–20, 22, 27, 28, 31, 34, 35, 37–40, 46–53 Average: 11–28, 30–32, 34–41, 43–53 Advanced: 12–14, 16–20, 22–30 even, 31, 32, 34–53

REACHING ALL LEARNERS – Differentiated Instruction for students with

Developing Knowledge	On-level Knowledge	Advanced Knowledge	English Language Development
☐ Inclusion TE p. 18	☐ Concrete Manipulatives TE p. 14	☐ Concrete Manipulatives TE p. 14	☐ Concrete Manipulatives TE p. 14
☐ Practice A 1-2 CRB	☐ Practice B 1-2 CRB	☐ Practice C 1-2 CRB	☐ Practice A, B, or C 1-2 CRB
☐ Reteach 1-2 CRB		☐ Challenge 1-2 CRB	☐ *Success for ELL* 1-2
☐ Homework Help Online Keyword: MR4 1-2	☐ Homework Help Online Keyword: MR4 1-2	☐ Homework Help Online Keyword: MR4 1-2	☐ Homework Help Online Keyword: MR4 1-2
☐ *Lesson Tutorial Video* 1-2	☐ *Lesson Tutorial Video* 1-2	☐ *Lesson Tutorial Video* 1-2	☐ *Lesson Tutorial Video* 1-2
☐ Reading Strategies 1-2 CRB	☐ Problem Solving 1-2 CRB	☐ Problem Solving 1-2 CRB	☐ Reading Strategies 1-2 CRB
☐ Questioning Strategies TE p. 14, 15, 16	☐ Critical Thinking TE p. 14	☐ Multiple Representations TE p. 18	☐ Vocabulary Exercises SE p. 13
☐ *IDEA Works!* 1-2			☐ *Multilingual Glossary*

ASSESSMENT
☐ Lesson Quiz, TE p. 19 and Transparency 1-2
☐ State-Specific Test Prep Online Keyword: MR4 TestPrep

Holt Geometry

Teacher's Name _____ Class _____ Date _____

Lesson Plan 1-3
Measuring and Constructing Angles pp. 20–27   Day _____

Objectives Name and classify angles. Measure and construct angles and angle bisectors.

NCTM Standards: students should understand meanings of operations and how they relate to one another.

Pacing
☐ 45-minute Classes: 1 day   ☐ 90-minute Classes: 1/2 day   ☐ Other_____

WARM UP
☐ Warm Up TE p. 20 and Warm Up Transparency 1-3
☐ Countdown to Testing Transparency, Week 1

TEACH
☐ Lesson Presentation CD-ROM 1-3
☐ Alternate Opener, Exploration Transparency 1-3, TE p. 20
☐ Reaching All Learners TE p. 21
☐ Additional Examples Transparencies 1-3
☐ Teaching Transparency 1-3
☐ *Geometry Lab Activities* 1-3
☐ *Know-It Notebook* 1-3

PRACTICE AND APPLY
☐ Examples 1-2: Basic: 11–14, 19–26, 33–35 Average 11–14, 19–27, 32–36 Advanced: 11–14, 19–27, 32–36
☐ Examples 1-4: Basic: 11–26, 29–31, 33–35, 38, 41–45, 51–58 Average: 11–37, 39–46, 48–58 Advanced: 11, 12–22 even, 23, 26–58

REACHING ALL LEARNERS – Differentiated Instruction for students with

Developing Knowledge	On-level Knowledge	Advanced Knowledge	English Language Development
☐ Inclusion TE p. 25	☐ Visual Cues TE p. 21	☐ Visual Cues TE p. 21	☐ Visual Cues TE p. 21
☐ Practice A 1-3 CRB	☐ Practice B 1-3 CRB	☐ Practice C 1-3 CRB	☐ Practice A, B, or C 1-3 CRB
☐ Reteach 1-3 CRB		☐ Challenge 1-3 CRB	☐ *Success for ELL* 1-3
☐ Homework Help Online Keyword: MR4 1-3	☐ Homework Help Online Keyword: MR4 1-3	☐ Homework Help Online Keyword: MR4 1-3	☐ Homework Help Online Keyword: MR4 1-3
☐ *Lesson Tutorial Video* 1-3	☐ *Lesson Tutorial Video* 1-3	☐ *Lesson Tutorial Video* 1-3	☐ *Lesson Tutorial Video* 1-3
☐ Reading Strategies 1-3 CRB	☐ Problem Solving 1-3 CRB	☐ Problem Solving 1-3 CRB	☐ Reading Strategies 1-3 CRB
☐ Questioning Strategies TE p. 21, 22, 23	☐ Reading Math TE p. 22, 23	☐ Visual TE p.22, 25, 26	☐ Vocabulary Exercises SE p.20
☐ *IDEA Works!* 1-3			☐ *Multilingual Glossary*

ASSESSMENT
☐ Lesson Quiz, TE p. 27 and Transparency 1-3
☐ State-Specific Test Prep Online Keyword: MR4 TestPrep

Holt Geometry

Teacher's Name _____ Class _____ Date _____

Lesson Plan 1-4

Pairs of Angles pp. 28–33   *Day* _____

Objectives Identify adjacent, vertical, complementary, and supplementary angles. Find measures of pairs of angles.

NCTM Standards: students should compute fluently and make reasonable estimates.

Pacing
☐ 45-minute Classes: 1 day   ☐ 90-minute Classes: 1/2 day ☐ Other_____

WARM UP
☐ Warm Up TE p. 28 and Warm Up Transparency 1-4
☐ Countdown to Testing Transparency, Week 1

TEACH
☐ Lesson Presentation CD-ROM 1-4
☐ Alternate Opener, Exploration Transparency 1-4, TE p. 28
☐ Reaching All Learners TE p. 29
☐ Additional Examples Transparencies 1-4
☐ Teaching Transparency 1-4
☐ *Know-It Notebook* 1-4

PRACTICE AND APPLY
☐ Examples 1-3: Basic: 14–22, 25, 27–30, 34 Average: 14–22, 25, 27–35 Advanced: 14–22, 25, 27–35, 37
☐ Examples 1-5: Basic: 14–22, 24–30, 33, 34, 37–43, 47–55 Average: 14–44, 47–55 Advanced: 14–55

REACHING ALL LEARNERS – Differentiated Instruction for students with

Developing Knowledge	On-level Knowledge	Advanced Knowledge	English Language Development
☐ Inclusion SE p. 30	☐ Cooperative Learning SE p. 29	☐ Cooperative Learning SE p. 29	☐ Cooperative Learning SE p. 29
☐ Practice A 1-4 CRB	☐ Practice B 1-4 CRB	☐ Practice C 1-4 CRB	☐ Practice A, B, or C 1-4 CRB
☐ Reteach 1-4 CRB		☐ Challenge 1-4 CRB	☐ *Success for ELL* 1-4
☐ Homework Help Online Keyword: MR4 1-4	☐ Homework Help Online Keyword: MR4 1-4	☐ Homework Help Online Keyword: MR4 1-4	☐ Homework Help Online Keyword: MR4 1-4
☐ *Lesson Tutorial Video* 1-4	☐ *Lesson Tutorial Video* 1-4	☐ *Lesson Tutorial Video* 1-4	☐ *Lesson Tutorial Video* 1-4
☐ Reading Strategies 1-4 CRB	☐ Problem Solving 1-4 CRB	☐ Problem Solving 1-4 CRB	☐ Reading Strategies 1-4 CRB
☐ Questioning Strategies TE p. 29, 30	☐ Cooperative Learning SE p. 29	☐ Visual TE p. 30	☐ Vocabulary Exercises SE p.28
☐ *IDEA Works!* 1-4			☐ *Multilingual Glossary*

ASSESSMENT
☐ Lesson Quiz, TE p. 33 and Transparency 1-4
☐ State-Specific Test Prep Online Keyword: MR4 TestPrep

Holt Geometry

Teacher's Name _____ Class _____ Date _____

Lesson Plan 1-5
Using Formulas in Geometry pp. 36–41   *Day* _____

Objective Apply formulas for perimeter, area, and circumference.

> **NCTM Standards:** students should use mathematical models to represent and understand quantitative relationships.

Pacing
☐ 45-minute Classes: 1 day   ☐ 90-minute Classes: 1/2 day   ☐ Other_____

WARM UP
☐ Warm Up TE p. 36 and Warm Up Transparency 1-5
☐ Countdown to Testing Transparency, Week 2

TEACH
☐ Lesson Presentation CD-ROM 1-5
☐ Alternate Opener, Exploration Transparency 1-5, TE p. 36
☐ Additional Examples Transparencies 1-5
☐ Teaching Transparency 1-5
☐ *Geometry Lab Activities* 1-5
☐ *Know-It Notebook* 1-5

PRACTICE AND APPLY
☐ Examples 1-3: Basic: 10–17, 19–24, 26–34 even, 38, 41, 42, 44, 46–50, 56–62 Average: 10–30, 32–52, 56–62 Advanced: 10–30 even, 31–62

REACHING ALL LEARNERS – Differentiated Instruction for students with

Developing Knowledge	On-level Knowledge	Advanced Knowledge	English Language Development
☐ Inclusion TE p. 36			
☐ Practice A 1-5 CRB	☐ Practice B 1-5 CRB	☐ Practice C 1-5 CRB	☐ Practice A, B, or C 1-5 CRB
☐ Reteach 1-5 CRB		☐ Challenge 1-5 CRB	☐ *Success for ELL* 1-5
☐ Homework Help Online Keyword: MR4 1-5	☐ Homework Help Online Keyword: MR4 1-5	☐ Homework Help Online Keyword: MR4 1-5	☐ Homework Help Online Keyword: MR4 1-5
☐ *Lesson Tutorial Video* 1-5	☐ *Lesson Tutorial Video* 1-5	☐ *Lesson Tutorial Video* 1-5	☐ *Lesson Tutorial Video* 1-5
☐ Reading Strategies 1-5 CRB	☐ Problem Solving 1-5 CRB	☐ Problem Solving 1-5 CRB	☐ Reading Strategies 1-5 CRB
☐ Questioning Strategies TE p. 37	☐ Number Sense TE p. 40	☐ Algebra TE p. 41	☐ Vocabulary Exercises SE p.36
☐ *IDEA Works!* 1-5			☐ *Multilingual Glossary*

ASSESSMENT
☐ Lesson Quiz, TE p. 41 and Transparency 1-5
☐ State-Specific Test Prep Online Keyword: MR4 TestPrep

Holt Geometry

Teacher's Name _____ Class _____ Date _____

Lesson Plan 1-6

Midpoint and Distance in the Coordinate Plane pp. 43-49   Day _____

Objective Develop and apply the formula for midpoint. Use the Distance Formula and the Pythagorean Theorem to find the distance between two points.

NCTM Standards: students should understand numbers, ways of representing numbers, relationships among numbers, and number systems.

Pacing
☐ 45-minute Classes: 1 day   ☐ 90-minute Classes: 1/2 day ☐ Other_____

WARM UP
☐ Warm Up TE p. 43 and Warm Up Transparency 1-6
☐ Countdown to Testing Transparency, Week 2

TEACH
☐ Lesson Presentation CD-ROM 1-6
☐ Alternate Opener, Exploration Transparency 1-6, TE p. 43
☐ Reaching All Learners TE p. 44
☐ Additional Examples Transparencies 1-6
☐ Teaching Transparency 1-6
☐ *Know-It Notebook* 1-6

PRACTICE AND APPLY
☐ Examples 1-3: Basic: 12–17, 22, 26, 27, 33 Average. 12–17, 22, 24–27, 33, 38 Advanced: 12–17, 22, 24–27, 33, 36, 38
☐ Examples 1-5: Basic: 12–23, 26–28, 30, 32–37, 42–50 Average: 12–39, 42–50 Advanced: 12–50

REACHING ALL LEARNERS – Differentiated Instruction for students with

Developing Knowledge	On-level Knowledge	Advanced Knowledge	English Language Development
☐ Inclusion TE p. 45	☐ Cognitive Strategies TE p. 44	☐ Cognitive Strategies TE p. 44	☐ Cognitive Strategies TE p. 44
☐ Practice A 1-6 CRB	☐ Practice B 1-6 CRB	☐ Practice C 1-6 CRB	☐ Practice A, B, or C 1-6 CRB
☐ Reteach 1-6 CRB		☐ Challenge 1-6 CRB	☐ *Success for ELL* 1-6
☐ Homework Help Online Keyword: MR4 1-6	☐ Homework Help Online Keyword: MR4 1-6	☐ Homework Help Online Keyword: MR4 1-6	☐ Homework Help Online Keyword: MR4 1-6
☐ *Lesson Tutorial Video* 1-6	☐ *Lesson Tutorial Video* 1-6	☐ *Lesson Tutorial Video* 1-6	☐ *Lesson Tutorial Video* 1-6
☐ Reading Strategies 1-6 CRB	☐ Problem Solving 1-6 CRB	☐ Problem Solving 1-6 CRB	☐ Reading Strategies 1-6 CRB
☐ Questioning Strategies TE p. 44, 45, 46	☐ Algebra TE p. 45	☐ Algebra TE p. 45	☐ Vocabulary Exercises SE p.43
☐ *IDEA Works!* 1-6			☐ *Multilingual Glossary*

ASSESSMENT
☐ Lesson Quiz, TE p. 49 and Transparency 1-6
☐ State-Specific Test Prep Online Keyword: MR4 TestPrep

Holt Geometry

Teacher's Name _____ Class _____ Date _____

Lesson Plan 1-7
Transformations in the Coordinate Plane pp. 50-55   *Day* _____

Objectives Identify reflections, rotations, and translations. Graph transformations in the coordinate plane.

NCTM Standards: students should specify locations and describe spatial relationships using coordinate geometry and other representational systems.

Pacing
☐ 45-minute Classes: 1 day   ☐ 90-minute Classes: 1/2 day   ☐ Other_____

WARM UP
☐ Warm Up TE p. 50 and Warm Up Transparency 1-7
☐ Countdown to Testing Transparency, Week 2

TEACH
☐ Lesson Presentation CD-ROM 1-7
☐ Alternate Opener, Exploration Transparency 1-7, TE p. 50
☐ Reaching All Learners TE p. 51
☐ Additional Examples Transparencies 1-7
☐ Teaching Transparency 1-7
☐ *Know-It Notebook* 1-7

PRACTICE AND APPLY
☐ Examples 1-2: Basic: 8–10, 13–15, 17–22 Average: 8–10, 13–15, 17–22 Advanced: 8–10, 13–15, 17–22, 34
☐ Examples 1-4: Basic: 8–18, 26–32, 38–47 Average: 8–33, 38–47 Advanced: 8–47

REACHING ALL LEARNERS – Differentiated Instruction for students with

Developing Knowledge	On-level Knowledge	Advanced Knowledge	English Language Development
☐ Inclusion TE p. 51	☐ Cognitive Strategies TE p. 51	☐ Cognitive Strategies TE p. 51	☐ Cognitive Strategies TE p. 51
☐ Practice A 1-7 CRB	☐ Practice B 1-7 CRB	☐ Practice C 1-7 CRB	☐ Practice A, B, or C 1-7 CRB
☐ Reteach 1-7 CRB		☐ Challenge 1-7 CRB	☐ *Success for ELL* 1-7
☐ Homework Help Online Keyword: MR4 1-7	☐ Homework Help Online Keyword: MR4 1-7	☐ Homework Help Online Keyword: MR4 1-7	☐ Homework Help Online Keyword: MR4 1-7
☐ *Lesson Tutorial Video* 1-7	☐ *Lesson Tutorial Video* 1-7	☐ *Lesson Tutorial Video* 1-7	☐ *Lesson Tutorial Video* 1-7
☐ Reading Strategies 1-7 CRB	☐ Problem Solving 1-7 CRB	☐ Problem Solving 1-7 CRB	☐ Reading Strategies 1-7 CRB
☐ Questioning Strategies TE p. 51, 52	☐ Communicating Math TE p. 54	☐ Communicating Math TE p. 54	☐ Vocabulary Exercises SE p. 50
☐ *IDEA Works!* 1-7			☐ *Multilingual Glossary*

ASSESSMENT
☐ Lesson Quiz, TE p. 55 and Transparency 1-7
☐ State-Specific Test Prep Online Keyword: MR4 TestPrep

Holt Geometry

Lesson Plan 2-1
Using Inductive Reasoning to Make Conjectures pp. 74–79   Day _____

Objectives Use inductive reasoning to identify patterns and make conjectures. Find counterexamples to disprove conjectures.

> **NCTM Standards:** students should use visualization, spatial reasoning, and geometric modeling to solve problems.

Pacing
☐ 45-minute Classes: 1 day   ☐ 90-minute Classes: 1/2 day ☐ Other_____

WARM UP
☐ Warm Up TE p. 74 and Warm Up Transparency 2-1
☐ Countdown to Testing Transparency, Week 3

TEACH
☐ Lesson Presentation CD-ROM 2-1
☐ Alternate Opener, Exploration Transparency 2-1, TE p. 74
☐ Reaching All Learners TE p. 75
☐ Additional Examples Transparencies 2-1
☐ *Know-It Notebook* 2-1

PRACTICE AND APPLY
☐ Examples 1-2: Basic: 11–15, 20–22, 31–33 Average: 11–15, 20–22, 28–33, 41 Advanced: 11–15, 20–23, 28–33, 41–43
☐ Examples 1-4: Basic: 11–27, 31–33, 36–39, 44–53 Average: 11–22, 24–29, 31, 32, 34–40, 44–53 Advanced: 12, 14, 16, 18, 20–53

REACHING ALL LEARNERS – Differentiated Instruction for students with

Developing Knowledge	On-level Knowledge	Advanced Knowledge	English Language Development
☐ Cooperative Learning TE p. 75	☐ Cooperative Learning TE p. 75	☐ Cooperative Learning TE p. 75	☐ Cooperative Learning TE p. 75
☐ Practice A 2-1 CRB	☐ Practice B 2-1 CRB	☐ Practice C 2-1 CRB	☐ Practice A, B, or C 2-1 CRB
☐ Reteach 2-1 CRB		☐ Challenge 2-1 CRB	☐ *Success for ELL* 2-1
☐ Homework Help Online Keyword: MR4 2-1	☐ Homework Help Online Keyword: MR4 2-1	☐ Homework Help Online Keyword: MR4 2-1	☐ Homework Help Online Keyword: MR4 2-1
☐ *Lesson Tutorial Video* 2-1	☐ *Lesson Tutorial Video* 2-1	☐ *Lesson Tutorial Video* 2-1	☐ *Lesson Tutorial Video* 2-1
☐ Reading *Strategies* 2-1 CRB	☐ Problem Solving 2-1 CRB	☐ Problem Solving 2-1 CRB	☐ Reading *Strategies* 2-1 CRB
☐ Questioning Strategies TE p. 75, 76	☐ Science TE p. 75	☐ Communicating Math TE p. 77	☐ Vocabulary Exercises SE p.74
☐ *IDEA Works!* 2-1			☐ *Multilingual Glossary*

ASSESSMENT
☐ Lesson Quiz, TE p. 79 and Transparency 2-1
☐ State-Specific Test Prep Online Keyword: MR4 TestPrep

Holt Geometry

Teacher's Name _____ Class _____ Date _____

Lesson Plan 2-2
Conditional Statements pp. 81–87   Day _____

Objectives Identify, write, and analyze the truth value of conditional statements. Write the inverse, converse, and contrapositive of a conditional statement.

> **NCTM Standards:** students should use mathematical models to represent and understand quantitative relationships.

Pacing
☐ 45-minute Classes: 1 day   ☐ 90-minute Classes: 1/2 day   ☐ Other_____

WARM UP
☐ Warm Up TE p. 81 and Warm Up Transparency 2-2
☐ Countdown to Testing Transparency, Week 3

TEACH
☐ Lesson Presentation CD-ROM 2-2
☐ Alternate Opener, Exploration Transparency 2-2, TE p. 81
☐ Reaching All Learners TE p. 82
☐ Additional Examples Transparencies 2-2
☐ Teaching Transparency 2-2
☐ *Geometry Lab Activities* 2-2
☐ *Know-It Notebook* 2-2

PRACTICE AND APPLY
☐ Examples 1-2: Basic: 13–18, 30–33 Average: 13–18, 30–36, 54 Advanced: 13–18, 30–36, 54–55
☐ Examples 1-4: Basic: 13–23, 30–37, 42–47, 49–53, 58–66 Average: 13–29, 36–55, 58–66 Advanced: 13–29, 36–66

REACHING ALL LEARNERS – Differentiated Instruction for students with

Developing Knowledge	On-level Knowledge	Advanced Knowledge	English Language Development
☐ Visual Cues TE p. 82	☐ Visual Cues TE p. 82	☐ Visual Cues TE p. 82	☐ Visual Cues TE p. 82
☐ Practice A 2-2 CRB	☐ Practice B 2-2 CRB	☐ Practice C 2-2 CRB	☐ Practice A, B, or C 2-2 CRB
☐ Reteach 2-2 CRB		☐ Challenge 2-2 CRB	☐ *Success for ELL* 2-2
☐ Homework Help Online Keyword: MR4 2-2	☐ Homework Help Online Keyword: MR4 2-2	☐ Homework Help Online Keyword: MR4 2-2	☐ Homework Help Online Keyword: MR4 2-2
☐ *Lesson Tutorial Video* 2-2	☐ *Lesson Tutorial Video* 2-2	☐ *Lesson Tutorial Video* 2-2	☐ *Lesson Tutorial Video* 2-2
☐ Reading Strategies 2-2 CRB	☐ Problem Solving 2-2 CRB	☐ Problem Solving 2-2 CRB	☐ Reading Strategies 2-2 CRB
☐ Questioning Strategies TE p. 82, 83	☐ Multiple Representations TE p. 82	☐ Critical Thinking TE p. 82	☐ Vocabulary Exercises SE p. 81
☐ *IDEA Works!* 2-2			☐ *Multilingual Glossary*

ASSESSMENT
☐ Lesson Quiz, TE p. 87 and Transparency 2-2
☐ State-Specific Test Prep Online Keyword: MR4 TestPrep

Holt Geometry

Lesson Plan 2-3
Using Deductive Reasoning to Verify Conjectures pp. 88–93   Day _____

Objective Apply the Law of Detachment and the Law of Syllogism in logical reasoning.

> **NCTM Standards:** students should use visualization, spatial reasoning, and geometric modeling to solve problems.

Pacing
☐ 45-minute Classes: 1 day   ☐ 90-minute Classes: 1/2 day   ☐ Other_____

WARM UP
☐ Warm Up TE p. 88 and Warm Up Transparency 2-3
☐ Countdown to Testing Transparency, Week 3

TEACH
☐ Lesson Presentation CD-ROM 2-3
☐ Alternate Opener, Exploration Transparency 2-3, TE p. 88
☐ Reaching All Learners TE p. 89
☐ Additional Examples Transparencies 2-3
☐ *Know-It Notebook* 2-3

PRACTICE AND APPLY
☐ Examples 1-2: Basic: 9–11 Average: 9–11, 14 Advanced: 9–11, 14
☐ Examples 1-4: Basic: 9–13, 15–18, 20, 22–25, 29–37 Average: 9–14, 16, 18–25, 28–37 Advanced: 9–14, 16, 18, 19, 21–37

REACHING ALL LEARNERS – Differentiated Instruction for students with

Developing Knowledge	On-level Knowledge	Advanced Knowledge	English Language Development
☐ Auditory Cues TE p. 89	☐ Auditory Cues TE p. 89	☐ Auditory Cues TE p. 89	☐ Auditory Cues TE p. 89
☐ Practice A 2-3 CRB	☐ Practice B 2-3 CRB	☐ Practice C 2-3 CRB	☐ Practice A, B, or C 2-3 CRB
☐ Reteach 2-3 CRB		☐ Challenge 2-3 CRB	☐ *Success for ELL* 2-3
☐ Homework Help Online Keyword: MR4 2-3	☐ Homework Help Online Keyword: MR4 2-3	☐ Homework Help Online Keyword: MR4 2-3	☐ Homework Help Online Keyword: MR4 2-3
☐ *Lesson Tutorial Video* 2-3	☐ *Lesson Tutorial Video* 2-3	☐ *Lesson Tutorial Video* 2-3	☐ *Lesson Tutorial Video* 2-3
☐ Reading Strategies 2-3 CRB	☐ Problem Solving 2-3 CRB	☐ Problem Solving 2-3 CRB	☐ Reading Strategies 2-3 CRB
☐ Questioning Strategies TE p. 89, 90	☐ Algebra TE p. 89	☐ Algebra TE p. 89	☐ Vocabulary Exercises SE p. 88
☐ *IDEA Works!* 2-3			☐ *Multilingual Glossary*

ASSESSMENT
☐ Lesson Quiz, TE p. 93 and Transparency 2-3
☐ State-Specific Test Prep Online Keyword: MR4 TestPrep

Holt Geometry

Teacher's Name _____ Class _____ Date _____

Lesson Plan 2-4
Biconditional Statements and Definitions pp. 96–101   Day _____

Objective Write and analyze biconditional statements.

NCTM Standards: students should select and use various types of reasoning and methods of proof.

Pacing
☐ 45-minute Classes: 1 day   ☐ 90-minute Classes: 1/2 day   ☐ Other_____

WARM UP
☐ Warm Up TE p. 96 and Warm Up Transparency 2-4
☐ Countdown to Testing Transparency, Week 3

TEACH
☐ Lesson Presentation CD-ROM 2-4
☐ Alternate Opener, Exploration Transparency 2-4, TE p. 96
☐ Reaching All Learners TE p. 97
☐ Additional Examples Transparencies 2-4
☐ Teaching Transparency 2-4
☐ *Geometry Lab Activities* 2-4
☐ *Know-It Notebook* 2-4

PRACTICE AND APPLY
☐ Examples 1-2: Basic: 10–15 Average: 10–15 Advanced: 10–15
☐ Examples 1-4: Basic: 10–21, 24, 28, 30–34, 37–41, 46–54 Average: 10–32, 35–41, 43–44, 46–54
    Advanced: 10–29, 30–34 even, 35–54

REACHING ALL LEARNERS – Differentiated Instruction for students with

Developing Knowledge	On-level Knowledge	Advanced Knowledge	English Language Development
☐ Inclusion TE p. 100	☐ Cooperative Learning p. 97	☐ Cooperative Learning p. 97	☐ Cooperative Learning p. 97
☐ Practice A 2-4 CRB	☐ Practice B 2-4 CRB	☐ Practice C 2-4 CRB	☐ Practice A, B, or C 2-4 CRB
☐ Reteach 2-4 CRB		☐ Challenge 2-4 CRB	☐ *Success for ELL* 2-4
☐ Homework Help Online Keyword: MR4 2-4	☐ Homework Help Online Keyword: MR4 2-4	☐ Homework Help Online Keyword: MR4 2-4	☐ Homework Help Online Keyword: MR4 2-4
☐ *Lesson Tutorial Video* 2-4	☐ *Lesson Tutorial Video* 2-4	☐ *Lesson Tutorial Video* 2-4	☐ *Lesson Tutorial Video* 2-4
☐ Reading Strategies 2-4 CRB	☐ Problem Solving 2-4 CRB	☐ Problem Solving 2-4 CRB	☐ Reading Strategies 2-4 CRB
☐ Questioning Strategies TE p. 97, 98	☐ Reading Math TE p. 98	☐ Reading Math TE p. 98	☐ Vocabulary Exercises SE p. 96
☐ *IDEA Works!* 2-4			☐ *Multilingual Glossary*

ASSESSMENT
☐ Lesson Quiz, TE p. 101 and Transparency 2-4
☐ State-Specific Test Prep Online Keyword: MR4 TestPrep

Holt Geometry

Teacher's Name _____ Class _____ Date _____

Lesson Plan 2-5
Algebraic Proof pp. 104–109   Day _____

Objectives Review properties of equality and use them to write algebraic proofs. Identify properties of equality and congruence.

NCTM Standards: students should analyze change in various contexts.

Pacing
☐ 45-minute Classes: 1 day   ☐ 90-minute Classes: 1/2 day   ☐ Other_____

WARM UP
☐ Warm Up TE p. 104 and Warm Up Transparency 2-5
☐ Countdown to Testing Transparency, Week 4

TEACH
☐ Lesson Presentation CD-ROM 2-5
☐ Alternate Opener, Exploration Transparency 2-5, TE p. 104
☐ Reaching All Learners TE p. 105
☐ Additional Examples Transparencies 2-5
☐ Teaching Transparency 2-5
☐ *Know-It Notebook* 2-5

PRACTICE AND APPLY
☐ Examples 1-2: Basic: 16–22, 33 Average: 16–22, 33–35 Advanced: 16–22, 29, 34, 35
☐ Examples 1-4: Basic: 16–28, 30–33, 37–42, 46–50 Average: 16–28, 30–34, 36–43, 45–50 Advanced: 16–29, 33–50

REACHING ALL LEARNERS – Differentiated Instruction for students with

Developing Knowledge	On-level Knowledge	Advanced Knowledge	English Language Development
☐ Kinesthetic Experience TE p. 105	☐ Kinesthetic Experience TE p. 105	☐ Kinesthetic Experience TE p. 105	☐ Kinesthetic Experience TE p. 105
☐ Practice A 2-5 CRB	☐ Practice B 2-5 CRB	☐ Practice C 2-5 CRB	☐ Practice A, B, or C 2-5 CRB
☐ Reteach 2-5 CRB		☐ Challenge 2-5 CRB	☐ *Success for ELL* 2-5
☐ Homework Help Online Keyword: MR4 2-5	☐ Homework Help Online Keyword: MR4 2-5	☐ Homework Help Online Keyword: MR4 2-5	☐ Homework Help Online Keyword: MR4 2-5
☐ *Lesson Tutorial Video* 2-5	☐ *Lesson Tutorial Video* 2-5	☐ *Lesson Tutorial Video* 2-5	☐ *Lesson Tutorial Video* 2-5
☐ Reading Strategies 2-5 CRB	☐ Problem Solving 2-5 CRB	☐ Problem Solving 2-5 CRB	☐ Reading Strategies 2-5 CRB
☐ Questioning Strategies TE p. 105, 106	☐ Visual TE p. 105	☐ Auditory TE p. 106	☐ Vocabulary Exercises SE p. 104
☐ *IDEA Works!* 2-5			☐ *Multilingual Glossary*

ASSESSMENT
☐ Lesson Quiz, TE p. 109 and Transparency 2-5
☐ State-Specific Test Prep Online Keyword: MR4 TestPrep

Holt Geometry

Teacher's Name _____ Class _____ Date _____

Lesson Plan 2-6
Geometric Proof pp. 110–116   Day _____

Objectives Write two-column proofs. Prove geometric theorems by using deductive reasoning.

> **NCTM Standards:** students should use visualization, spatial reasoning, and geometric modeling to solve problems.

Pacing
☐ 45-minute Classes: 1 day   ☐ 90-minute Classes: 1/2 day   ☐ Other_____

WARM UP
☐ Warm Up TE p. 110 and Warm Up Transparency 2-6
☐ Countdown to Testing Transparency, Week 4

TEACH
☐ Lesson Presentation CD-ROM 2-6
☐ Alternate Opener, Exploration Transparency 2-6, TE p. 110
☐ Reaching All Learners TE p. 111
☐ Additional Examples Transparencies 2-6
☐ Teaching Transparency 2-6
☐ *Know-It Notebook* 2-6

PRACTICE AND APPLY
☐ Examples 1-2: Basic: 6–8, 12 Average: 6–8, 11, 12, 14 Advanced: 6–8, 11, 12–22 even
☐ Examples 1-3: Basic: 6–12, 16–20, 22–27, 31–36 Average: 6–16, 18–22 even, 23–27, 31–36
    Advanced: 6–16, 18, 21–36

REACHING ALL LEARNERS – Differentiated Instruction for students with

Developing Knowledge	On-level Knowledge	Advanced Knowledge	English Language Development
☐ Inclusion TE p. 112	☐ Critical Thinking TE p. 111	☐ Critical Thinking TE p. 111	☐ Critical Thinking TE p. 111
☐ Practice A 2-6 CRB	☐ Practice B 2-6 CRB	☐ Practice C 2-6 CRB	☐ Practice A, B, or C 2-6 CRB
☐ Reteach 2-6 CRB		☐ Challenge 2-6 CRB	☐ *Success for ELL* 2-6
☐ Homework Help Online Keyword: MR4 2-6	☐ Homework Help Online Keyword: MR4 2-6	☐ Homework Help Online Keyword: MR4 2-6	☐ Homework Help Online Keyword: MR4 2-6
☐ *Lesson Tutorial Video* 2-6	☐ *Lesson Tutorial Video* 2-6	☐ *Lesson Tutorial Video* 2-6	☐ *Lesson Tutorial Video* 2-6
☐ Reading Strategies 2-6 CRB	☐ Problem Solving 2-6 CRB	☐ Problem Solving 2-6 CRB	☐ Reading Strategies 2-6 CRB
☐ Questioning Strategies TE p. 111, 112	☐ Auditory TE p. 111	☐ Communicating Math TE p. 115	☐ Vocabulary Exercises SE p. 110
☐ *IDEA Works!* 2-6			☐ *Multilingual Glossary*

ASSESSMENT
☐ Lesson Quiz, TE p. 116 and Transparency 2-6
☐ State-Specific Test Prep Online Keyword: MR4 TestPrep

Teacher's Name _____ Class _____ Date _____

Lesson Plan 2-7
Flowchart and Paragraph Proofs pp. 118–125   Day _____

Objectives Write flowchart and paragraph proofs. Prove geometric theorems by using deductive reasoning.

> **NCTM Standards:** students should formulate questions that can be addressed with data and collect, organize, and display relevant data to answer them.

Pacing
☐ 45-minute Classes: 1 day   ☐ 90-minute Classes: 1/2 day   ☐ Other_____

WARM UP
☐ Warm Up TE p. 118 and Warm Up Transparency 2-7
☐ Countdown to Testing Transparency, Week 4

TEACH
☐ Lesson Presentation CD-ROM 2-7
☐ Alternate Opener, Exploration Transparency 2-7, TE p. 118
☐ Reaching All Learners TE p. 119
☐ Additional Examples Transparencies 2-7
☐ Teaching Transparency 2-7
☐ *Technology Lab Activities* 2-7
☐ *Know-It Notebook* 2-7

PRACTICE AND APPLY
☐ Examples 1-2: Basic: 7, 8, 12–16 Average: 7, 8, 11, 12–16 even Advanced: 7, 8, 11–16
☐ Examples 1-4: Basic: 7–18, 20–23, 28–36 Average: 7–10, 12–16 even, 17–23, 26–36 Advanced: 7–10, 12–16 even, 18–36

REACHING ALL LEARNERS – Differentiated Instruction for students with

Developing Knowledge	On-level Knowledge	Advanced Knowledge	English Language Development
☐ Visual Cues TE p. 119	☐ Visual Cues TE p. 119	☐ Visual Cues TE p. 119	☐ Visual Cues TE p. 119
☐ Practice A 2-7 CRB	☐ Practice B 2-7 CRB	☐ Practice C 2-7 CRB	☐ Practice A, B, or C 2-7 CRB
☐ Reteach 2-7 CRB		☐ Challenge 2-7 CRB	☐ *Success for ELL* 2-7
☐ Homework Help Online Keyword: MR4 2-7	☐ Homework Help Online Keyword: MR4 2-7	☐ Homework Help Online Keyword: MR4 2-7	☐ Homework Help Online Keyword: MR4 2-7
☐ *Lesson Tutorial Video* 2-7	☐ *Lesson Tutorial Video* 2-7	☐ *Lesson Tutorial Video* 2-7	☐ *Lesson Tutorial Video* 2-7
☐ Reading Strategies 2-7 CRB	☐ Problem Solving 2-7 CRB	☐ Problem Solving 2-7 CRB	☐ Reading Strategies 2-7 CRB
☐ Questioning Strategies TE p. 119, 120, 121	☐ Reading Math TE p. 123	☐ Multiple Representations TE p. 119	☐ Vocabulary Exercises SE p. 118
☐ *IDEA Works!* 2-7			☐ *Multilingual Glossary*

ASSESSMENT
☐ Lesson Quiz, TE p. 125 and Transparency 2-7
☐ State-Specific Test Prep Online Keyword: MR4 TestPrep

Holt Geometry

Teacher's Name _____ Class _____ Date _____

Lesson Plan 3-1
Lines and Angles pp. 146–151 Day _____

Objectives Identify parallel, perpendicular, and skew lines. Identify the angles formed by two lines and a transversal.

> **NCTM Standards:** students should understand numbers, ways of representing numbers, relationships among numbers, and number systems.

Pacing
☐ 45-minute Classes: 1 day   ☐ 90-minute Classes: 1/2 day   ☐ Other_____

WARM UP
☐ Warm Up TE p. 146 and Warm Up Transparency 3-1
☐ Countdown to Testing Transparency, Week 5

TEACH
☐ Lesson Presentation CD-ROM 3-1
☐ Alternate Opener, Exploration Transparency 3-1, TE p. 146
☐ Additional Examples Transparencies 3-1
☐ Teaching Transparency 3-1
☐ *Know-It Notebook* 3-1

PRACTICE AND APPLY
☐ Examples 1-3: Basic: 14–29, 33, 35–37, 43–48, 55–62 Average: 14–24 even, 26–52, 55–62
   Advanced: 14–24 even, 26–34, 41–62

REACHING ALL LEARNERS – Differentiated Instruction for students with

Developing Knowledge	On-level Knowledge	Advanced Knowledge	English Language Development
☐ Inclusion TE p. 148			
☐ Practice A 3-1 CRB	☐ Practice B 3-1 CRB	☐ Practice C 3-1 CRB	☐ Practice A, B, or C 3-1 CRB
☐ Reteach 3-1 CRB		☐ Challenge 3-1 CRB	☐ *Success for ELL* 3-1
☐ Homework Help Online Keyword: MR4 3-1	☐ Homework Help Online Keyword: MR4 3-1	☐ Homework Help Online Keyword: MR4 3-1	☐ Homework Help Online Keyword: MR4 3-1
☐ *Lesson Tutorial Video* 3-1	☐ *Lesson Tutorial Video* 3-1	☐ *Lesson Tutorial Video* 3-1	☐ *Lesson Tutorial Video* 3-1
☐ Reading *Strategies* 3-1 CRB	☐ Problem Solving 3-1 CRB	☐ Problem Solving 3-1 CRB	☐ Reading *Strategies* 3-1 CRB
☐ Questioning Strategies TE p. 147	☐ Kinesthetic TE p. 149	☐ Reading Math TE p. 147	☐ Vocabulary Exercises SE p. 146
☐ *IDEA Works!* 3-1			☐ *Multilingual Glossary*

ASSESSMENT
☐ Lesson Quiz, TE p. 151 and Transparency 3-1
☐ State-Specific Test Prep Online Keyword: MR4 TestPrep

Holt Geometry

Lesson Plan 3-2

Angles Formed by Parallel Lines and Transversals pp. 155–161   *Day* _____

Objective Prove and use theorems about the angles formed by parallel lines and a transversal.

> **NCTM Standards:** students should develop and evaluate inferences and predictions that are based on data.

Pacing
☐ 45-minute Classes: 1 day   ☐ 90-minute Classes: 1/2 day ☐ Other_____

WARM UP
☐ Warm Up TE p. 155 and Warm Up Transparency 3-2
☐ Countdown to Testing Transparency, Week 5

TEACH
☐ Lesson Presentation CD-ROM 3-2
☐ Alternate Opener, Exploration Transparency 3-2, TE p. 155
☐ Reaching All Learners TE p. 156
☐ Additional Examples Transparencies 3-2
☐ Teaching Transparency 3-2
☐ *Geometry Lab Activities* 3-2
☐ *Know-It Notebook* 3-2

PRACTICE AND APPLY
☐ Examples 1-3: Basic: 6–25, 29, 31, 33–36, 41–47 Average: 6–12, 13–19 even, 20–38, 41–47
　　Advanced: 6–12, 13–19 even, 20–30, 32–47

REACHING ALL LEARNERS – Differentiated Instruction for students with

Developing Knowledge	On-level Knowledge	Advanced Knowledge	English Language Development
☐ Kinesthetic Experience TE p. 156	☐ Kinesthetic Experience TE p. 156	☐ Kinesthetic Experience TE p. 156	☐ Kinesthetic Experience TE p. 156
☐ Practice A 3-2 CRB	☐ Practice B 3-2 CRB	☐ Practice C 3-2 CRB	☐ Practice A, B, or C 3-2 CRB
☐ Reteach 3-2 CRB		☐ Challenge 3-2 CRB	☐ *Success for ELL* 3-2
☐ Homework Help Online Keyword: MR4 3-2	☐ Homework Help Online Keyword: MR4 3-2	☐ Homework Help Online Keyword: MR4 3-2	☐ Homework Help Online Keyword: MR4 3-2
☐ *Lesson Tutorial Video* 3-2	☐ *Lesson Tutorial Video* 3-2	☐ *Lesson Tutorial Video* 3-2	☐ *Lesson Tutorial Video* 3-2
☐ Reading Strategies 3-2 CRB	☐ Problem Solving 3-2 CRB	☐ Problem Solving 3-2 CRB	☐ Reading Strategies 3-2 CRB
☐ Questioning Strategies TE p. 156, 157	☐ Multiple Representations TE p. 156	☐ Algebra TE p. 158	
☐ *IDEA Works!* 3-2			☐ *Multilingual Glossary*

ASSESSMENT
☐ Lesson Quiz, TE p. 161 and Transparency 3-2
☐ State-Specific Test Prep Online Keyword: MR4 TestPrep

Holt Geometry

Teacher's Name _____ Class _____ Date _____

Lesson Plan 3-3
Proving Lines Parallel pp. 162–169   Day _____

Objective Use the angles formed by a transversal to prove two lines are parallel.

NCTM Standards: students should use visualization, spatial reasoning, and geometric modeling to solve problems.

Pacing
☐ 45-minute Classes: 1 day   ☐ 90-minute Classes: 1/2 day   ☐ Other_____

WARM UP
☐ Warm Up TE p. 162 and Warm Up Transparency 3-3
☐ Countdown to Testing Transparency, Week 5

TEACH
☐ Lesson Presentation CD-ROM 3-3
☐ Alternate Opener, Exploration Transparency 3-3, TE p. 162
☐ Reaching All Learners TE p. 163
☐ Additional Examples Transparencies 3-3
☐ Teaching Transparency 3-3
☐ *Know-It Notebook* 3-3

PRACTICE AND APPLY
☐ Examples 1-2: Basic: 12–20, 24–34 even Average: 12–20, 24–34 Advanced: 12–20, 24–35
☐ Examples 1-4: Basic: 12–21, 24–36 even, 37, 40, 42–45, 57–65 Average: 12–22 even, 25–53, 57–65
    Advanced: 12–36 even, 37–65

REACHING ALL LEARNERS – Differentiated Instruction for students with

Developing Knowledge	On-level Knowledge	Advanced Knowledge	English Language Development
☐ Concrete Manipulatives TE p. 163	☐ Concrete Manipulatives TE p. 163	☐ Concrete Manipulatives TE p. 163	☐ Concrete Manipulatives TE p. 163
☐ Practice A 3-3 CRB	☐ Practice B 3-3 CRB	☐ Practice C 3-3 CRB	☐ Practice A, B, or C 3-3 CRB
☐ Reteach 3-3 CRB		☐ Challenge 3-3 CRB	☐ *Success for ELL* 3-3
☐ Homework Help Online Keyword: MR4 3-3	☐ Homework Help Online Keyword: MR4 3-3	☐ Homework Help Online Keyword: MR4 3-3	☐ Homework Help Online Keyword: MR4 3-3
☐ *Lesson Tutorial Video* 3-3	☐ *Lesson Tutorial Video* 3-3	☐ *Lesson Tutorial Video* 3-3	☐ *Lesson Tutorial Video* 3-3
☐ Reading Strategies 3-3 CRB	☐ Problem Solving 3-3 CRB	☐ Problem Solving 3-3 CRB	☐ Reading Strategies 3-3 CRB
☐ Questioning Strategies TE p. 163, 164, 165	☐ Reading Math TE p. 165	☐ Algebra TE p. 167	
☐ *IDEA Works!* 3-3			☐ *Multilingual Glossary*

ASSESSMENT
☐ Lesson Quiz, TE p. 169 and Transparency 3-3
☐ State-Specific Test Prep Online Keyword: MR4 TestPrep

Holt Geometry

Teacher's Name _____ Class _____ Date _____

Lesson Plan 3-4
Perpendicular Lines pp. 172–178   Day _____

Objective Prove and apply theorems about perpendicular lines.

> **NCTM Standards:** students should understand meanings of operations and how they relate to one another.

Pacing
☐ 45-minute Classes: 1 day   ☐ 90-minute Classes: 1/2 day   ☐ Other_____

WARM UP
☐ Warm Up TE p. 172 and Warm Up Transparency 3-4
☐ Countdown to Testing Transparency, Week 6

TEACH
☐ Lesson Presentation CD-ROM 3-4
☐ Alternate Opener, Exploration Transparency 3-4, TE p. 172
☐ Reaching All Learners TE p. 173
☐ Additional Examples Transparencies 3-4
☐ Teaching Transparency 3-4
☐ *Geometry Lab Activities* 3-4
☐ *Know-It Notebook* 3-4

PRACTICE AND APPLY
☐ Examples 1-3: Basic: 6–9, 10–20 even, 23–24, 27–28, 31–35, 39–45 Average: 6–26, 28–36, 39–45
   Advanced: 6–23, 25–45

REACHING ALL LEARNERS – Differentiated Instruction for students with

Developing Knowledge	On-level Knowledge	Advanced Knowledge	English Language Development
☐ Inclusion TE p. 176	☐ Modeling TE p. 173	☐ Modeling TE p. 173	☐ Modeling TE p. 173
☐ Practice A 3-4 CRB	☐ Practice B 3-4 CRB	☐ Practice C 3-4 CRB	☐ Practice A, B, or C 3-4 CRB
☐ Reteach 3-4 CRB		☐ Challenge 3-4 CRB	☐ *Success for ELL* 3-4
☐ Homework Help Online Keyword: MR4 3-4	☐ Homework Help Online Keyword: MR4 3-4	☐ Homework Help Online Keyword: MR4 3-4	☐ Homework Help Online Keyword: MR4 3-4
☐ *Lesson Tutorial Video* 3-4	☐ *Lesson Tutorial Video* 3-4	☐ *Lesson Tutorial Video* 3-4	☐ *Lesson Tutorial Video* 3-4
☐ Reading Strategies 3-4 CRB	☐ Problem Solving 3-4 CRB	☐ Problem Solving 3-4 CRB	☐ Reading Strategies 3-4 CRB
☐ Questioning Strategies TE p. 173	☐ Algebra TE p. 176	☐ Critical Thinking TE p. 175	☐ Vocabulary Exercises SÉ p. 172
☐ *IDEA Works!* 3-4			☐ *Multilingual Glossary*

ASSESSMENT
☐ Lesson Quiz, TE p. 178 and Transparency 3-4
☐ State-Specific Test Prep Online Keyword: MR4 TestPrep

Holt Geometry

Teacher's Name _____ Class _____ Date _____

Lesson Plan 3-5
Slopes of Lines pp. 182–187   Day _____

Objectives Find the slope of a line. Use slopes to identify parallel and perpendicular lines.

NCTM Standards: students should use visualization, spatial reasoning, and geometric modeling to solve problems.

Pacing
☐ 45-minute Classes: 1 day   ☐ 90-minute Classes: 1/2 day   ☐ Other_____

WARM UP
☐ Warm Up TE p. 182 and Warm Up Transparency 3-5
☐ Countdown to Testing Transparency, Week 6

TEACH
☐ Lesson Presentation CD-ROM 3-5
☐ Alternate Opener, Exploration Transparency 3-5, TE p. 182
☐ Reaching All Learners TE p. 183
☐ Additional Examples Transparencies 3-5
☐ Teaching Transparency 3-5
☐ *Geometry Lab Activities* 3-5
☐ *Know-It Notebook* 3-5

PRACTICE AND APPLY
☐ Examples 1-3: Basic: 10–14, 16–22 even, 24–28, 34–40 Average: 10–14, 16–22 even, 23–30, 34–40
   Advanced: 10–14 even, 15–40

REACHING ALL LEARNERS – Differentiated Instruction for students with

Developing Knowledge	On-level Knowledge	Advanced Knowledge	English Language Development
☐ Inclusion TE p. 186	☐ Kinesthetic Experience TE p. 183	☐ Kinesthetic Experience TE p. 183	☐ Kinesthetic Experience TE p. 183
☐ Practice A 3-5 CRB	☐ Practice B 3-5 CRB	☐ Practice C 3-5 CRB	☐ Practice A, B, or C 3-5 CRB
☐ Reteach 3-5 CRB		☐ Challenge 3-5 CRB	☐ *Success for ELL* 3-5
☐ Homework Help Online Keyword: MR4 3-5	☐ Homework Help Online Keyword: MR4 3-5	☐ Homework Help Online Keyword: MR4 3-5	☐ Homework Help Online Keyword: MR4 3-5
☐ *Lesson Tutorial Video* 3-5	☐ *Lesson Tutorial Video* 3-5	☐ *Lesson Tutorial Video* 3-5	☐ *Lesson Tutorial Video* 3-5
☐ Reading Strategies 3-5 CRB	☐ Problem Solving 3-5 CRB	☐ Problem Solving 3-5 CRB	☐ Reading Strategies 3-5 CRB
☐ Questioning Strategies TE p. 183, 184	☐ Science Link TE p. 185	☐ Science Link TE p. 185	☐ Vocabulary Exercises SE p. 182
☐ *IDEA Works!* 3-5			☐ *Multilingual Glossary*

ASSESSMENT
☐ Lesson Quiz, TE p. 187 and Transparency 3-5
☐ State-Specific Test Prep Online Keyword: MR4 TestPrep

Holt Geometry

Lesson Plan 3-6
Lines in the Coordinate Plane pp. 190–197 Day _____

Objectives Graph lines and write their equations in slope-intercept and point-slope form. Classify lines as parallel, intersecting, or coinciding.

> **NCTM Standards:** students should specify locations and describe spatial relationships using coordinate geometry and other representational systems.

Pacing
☐ 45-minute Classes: 1 day   ☐ 90-minute Classes: 1/2 day   ☐ Other_____

WARM UP
☐ Warm Up TE p. 190 and Warm Up Transparency 3-6
☐ Countdown to Testing Transparency, Week 6

TEACH
☐ Lesson Presentation CD-ROM 3-6
☐ Alternate Opener, Exploration Transparency 3-6, TE p. 190
☐ Reaching All Learners TE p. 191
☐ Additional Examples Transparencies 3-6
☐ Teaching Transparency 3-6
☐ *Technology Lab Activities* 3-6
☐ *Know-It Notebook* 3-6

PRACTICE AND APPLY
☐ Examples 1-2: Basic: 13–18, 24–30 Average: 13–18, 24–31 Advanced: 13–18, 24–31, 46
☐ Examples 1-4: Basic: 12–23, 24–44 even, 45–46, 53, 57–61, 67–73 Average: 13–23 even, 24–31, 32–44 even, 46–52 even, 53–54, 56–64, 67–73 Advanced: 12–23, 24–44 even, 47–52 even, 53–73

REACHING ALL LEARNERS – Differentiated Instruction for students with

Developing Knowledge	On-level Knowledge	Advanced Knowledge	English Language Development
☐ Inclusion TE p. 195	☐ Curriculum Integration TE p. 191	☐ Curriculum Integration TE p. 191	☐ Curriculum Integration TE p. 191
☐ Practice A 3-6 CRB	☐ Practice B 3-6 CRB	☐ Practice C 3-6 CRB	☐ Practice A, B, or C 3-6 CRB
☐ Reteach 3-6 CRB		☐ Challenge 3-6 CRB	☐ *Success for ELL* 3-6
☐ Homework Help Online Keyword: MR4 3-6	☐ Homework Help Online Keyword: MR4 3-6	☐ Homework Help Online Keyword: MR4 3-6	☐ Homework Help Online Keyword: MR4 3-6
☐ *Lesson Tutorial Video* 3-6	☐ *Lesson Tutorial Video* 3-6	☐ *Lesson Tutorial Video* 3-6	☐ *Lesson Tutorial Video* 3-6
☐ Reading Strategies 3-6 CRB	☐ Problem Solving 3-6 CRB	☐ Problem Solving 3-6 CRB	☐ Reading Strategies 3-6 CRB
☐ Questioning Strategies TE p. 191, 192, 193			☐ Vocabulary Exercises SE p. 190
☐ *IDEA Works!* 3-6			☐ *Multilingual Glossary*

ASSESSMENT
☐ Lesson Quiz, TE p. 197 and Transparency 3-6
☐ State-Specific Test Prep Online Keyword: MR4 TestPrep

Holt Geometry

Teacher's Name _____ Class _____ Date _____

Lesson Plan 4-1
Classifying Triangles pp. 216–221   Day _____

Objectives Classify triangles by their angle measures and side lengths. Use triangle classification to find angle measures and side lengths.

> **NCTM Standards:** students should understand numbers, ways of representing numbers, relationships among numbers, and number systems.

Pacing
☐ 45-minute Classes: 1 day   ☐ 90-minute Classes: 1/2 day   ☐ Other_____

WARM UP
☐ Warm Up TE p. 216 and Warm Up Transparency 4-1
☐ Countdown to Testing Transparency, Week 7

TEACH
☐ Lesson Presentation CD-ROM 4-1
☐ Alternate Opener, Exploration Transparency 4-1, TE p. 216
☐ Reaching All Learners TE p. 217
☐ Additional Examples Transparencies 4-1
☐ Teaching Transparency 4-1
☐ *Know-It Notebook* 4-1

PRACTICE AND APPLY
☐ Examples 1–2: Basic: 12–17, 20, 23–31, 35–37 Average: 12–17, 20, 23–31, 35–37, 39 Advanced: 12–17, 20, 23–31, 35–37, 39, 46
☐ Examples 1–4: Basic: 12–29, 35, 36, 39–44, 49–58 Average: 12–23, 24–32 even, 33, 34, 38–44, 48–58 Advanced: 12–22, 24–30 even, 32–34, 38–58

REACHING ALL LEARNERS – Differentiated Instruction for students with

Developing Knowledge	On-level Knowledge	Advanced Knowledge	English Language Development
☐ Inclusion TE p. 217	☐ Auditory Cues TE p. 217	☐ Auditory Cues TE p. 217	☐ Auditory Cues TE p. 217
☐ Practice A 4-1 CRB	☐ Practice B 4-1 CRB	☐ Practice C 4-1 CRB	☐ Practice A, B, or C 4-1 CRB
☐ Reteach 4-1 CRB		☐ Challenge 4-1 CRB	☐ *Success for ELL* 4-1
☐ Homework Help Online Keyword: MR4 4-1	☐ Homework Help Online Keyword: MR4 4-1	☐ Homework Help Online Keyword: MR4 4-1	☐ Homework Help Online Keyword: MR4 4-1
☐ *Lesson Tutorial Video* 4-1	☐ *Lesson Tutorial Video* 4-1	☐ *Lesson Tutorial Video* 4-1	☐ *Lesson Tutorial Video* 4-1
☐ Reading *Strategies* 4-1 CRB	☐ Problem Solving 4-1 CRB	☐ Problem Solving 4-1 CRB	☐ Reading *Strategies* 4-1 CRB
☐ Questioning Strategies TE p. 217, 218	☐ Visual TE p. 219	☐ Algebra TE p. 217	☐ Vocabulary Exercises SE p. 216
☐ *IDEA Works!* 4-1			☐ *Multilingual Glossary*

ASSESSMENT
☐ Lesson Quiz, TE p. 221 and Transparency 4-1
☐ State-Specific Test Prep Online Keyword: MR4 TestPrep

Holt Geometry

Teacher's Name _____ Class _____ Date _____

Lesson Plan 4-2
Angle Relationships in Triangles pp. 223-230   Day _____

Objectives Find the measures of interior and exterior angles of triangles. Apply theorems about the interior and exterior angles of triangles.

NCTM Standards: students should compute fluently and make reasonable estimates.

Pacing
☐ 45-minute Classes: 1 day   ☐ 90-minute Classes: 1/2 day   ☐ Other_____

WARM UP
☐ Warm Up TE p. 223 and Warm Up Transparency 4-2
☐ Countdown to Testing Transparency, Week 7

TEACH
☐ Lesson Presentation CD-ROM 4-2
☐ Alternate Opener, Exploration Transparency 4-2, TE p. 223
☐ Reaching All Learners TE p. 224
☐ Additional Examples Transparencies 4-2
☐ Teaching Transparency 4-2
☐ *Technology Lab Activities* 4-2
☐ *Know-It Notebook* 4-2

PRACTICE AND APPLY
☐ Examples 1-2: Basic: 15–18, 23, 24, 29–31, 35 Average: 15–18, 23–26, 29–31, 35 Advanced: 15–18, 23–26, 29–31, 35, 46, 48, 49
☐ Examples 1-4: Basic: 15–24, 29–32, 35, 40–44, 50–57 Average: 15–24, 29–35, 38–44, 49–57 Advanced: 15–29, 33–57

REACHING ALL LEARNERS – Differentiated Instruction for students with

Developing Knowledge	On-level Knowledge	Advanced Knowledge	English Language Development
☐ Modeling TE p. 224	☐ Modeling TE p. 224	☐ Modeling TE p. 224	☐ Modeling TE p. 224
☐ Practice A 4-2 CRB	☐ Practice B 4-2 CRB	☐ Practice C 4-2 CRB	☐ Practice A, B, or C 4-2 CRB
☐ Reteach 4-2 CRB		☐ Challenge 4-2 CRB	☐ *Success for ELL* 4-2
☐ Homework Help Online Keyword: MR4 4-2	☐ Homework Help Online Keyword: MR4 4-2	☐ Homework Help Online Keyword: MR4 4-2	☐ Homework Help Online Keyword: MR4 4-2
☐ *Lesson Tutorial Video* 4-2	☐ *Lesson Tutorial Video* 4-2	☐ *Lesson Tutorial Video* 4-2	☐ *Lesson Tutorial Video* 4-2
☐ Reading Strategies 4-2 CRB	☐ Problem Solving 4-2 CRB	☐ Problem Solving 4-2 CRB	☐ Reading Strategies 4-2 CRB
☐ Questioning Strategies TE p. 224, 225, 226	☐ Language Arts TE p. 224	☐ Algebra TE p. 228	☐ Vocabulary Exercises SE p. 223
☐ *IDEA Works!* 4-2			☐ *Multilingual Glossary*

ASSESSMENT
☐ Lesson Quiz, TE p. 230 and Transparency 4-2
☐ State-Specific Test Prep Online Keyword: MR4 TestPrep

Holt Geometry

Lesson Plan 4-3

Congruent Triangles pp. 231–237   *Day* _____

Objectives Use properties of congruent triangles. Prove triangles congruent by using the definition of congruence.

> **NCTM Standards:** students should understand meanings of operations and how they relate to one another.

Pacing
☐ 45-minute Classes: 1 day   ☐ 90-minute Classes: 1/2 day   ☐ Other_____

WARM UP
☐ Warm Up TE p. 231 and Warm Up Transparency 4-3
☐ Countdown to Testing Transparency, Week 7

TEACH
☐ Lesson Presentation CD-ROM 4-3
☐ Alternate Opener, Exploration Transparency 4-3, TE p. 231
☐ Reaching All Learners TE p. 232
☐ Additional Examples Transparencies 4-3
☐ Teaching Transparency 4-3
☐ *Know-It Notebook* 4-3

PRACTICE AND APPLY
☐ Examples 1-2: Basic: 13–18, 21, 23–25 Average: 13–18, 21, 22–25 Advanced: 13–18, 21, 22–25, 36
☐ Examples 1-4: Basic: 13–20, 23–26, 29, 31–34, 38–45 Average: 13–26, 28–35, 38–45 Advanced: 13–20, 22–28, 30–45

REACHING ALL LEARNERS – Differentiated Instruction for students with

Developing Knowledge	On-level Knowledge	Advanced Knowledge	English Language Development
☐ Inclusion TE p. 235	☐ Visual Cues TE p. 232	☐ Visual Cues TE p. 232	☐ Visual Cues TE p. 232
☐ Practice A 4-3 CRB	☐ Practice B 4-3 CRB	☐ Practice C 4-3 CRB	☐ Practice A, B, or C 4-3 CRB
☐ Reteach 4-3 CRB		☐ Challenge 4-3 CRB	☐ *Success for ELL* 4-3
☐ Homework Help Online Keyword: MR4 4-3	☐ Homework Help Online Keyword: MR4 4-3	☐ Homework Help Online Keyword: MR4 4-3	☐ Homework Help Online Keyword: MR4 4-3
☐ *Lesson Tutorial Video* 4-3	☐ *Lesson Tutorial Video* 4-3	☐ *Lesson Tutorial Video* 4-3	☐ *Lesson Tutorial Video* 4-3
☐ Reading Strategies 4-3 CRB	☐ Problem Solving 4-3 CRB	☐ Problem Solving 4-3 CRB	☐ Reading Strategies 4-3 CRB
☐ Questioning Strategies TE p. 232, 233	☐ Reading Math TE p. 232	☐ Visual TE p. 235, 237	☐ Vocabulary Exercises SE p. 231
☐ *IDEA Works!* 4-3			☐ *Multilingual Glossary*

ASSESSMENT
☐ Lesson Quiz, TE p. 237 and Transparency 4-3
☐ State-Specific Test Prep Online Keyword: MR4 TestPrep

Holt Geometry

Lesson Plan 4-4

Triangle Congruence: SSS and SAS pp. 242–249   Day _____

Objectives Apply SSS and SAS to construct triangles and to solve problems. Prove triangles congruent by using SSS and SAS.

> **NCTM Standards:** students should apply appropriate techniques, tools, and formulas to determine measurements.

Pacing
☐ 45-minute Classes: 1 day   ☐ 90-minute Classes: 1/2 day ☐ Other_____

WARM UP
☐ Warm Up TE p. 242 and Warm Up Transparency 4-4
☐ Countdown to Testing Transparency, Week 8

TEACH
☐ Lesson Presentation CD-ROM 4-4
☐ Alternate Opener, Exploration Transparency 4-4, TE p. 242
☐ Reaching All Learners TE p. 243
☐ Additional Examples Transparencies 4-4
☐ Teaching Transparency 4-4
☐ *Geometry Lab Activities* 4-4
☐ *Know-It Notebook* 4-4

PRACTICE AND APPLY
☐ Examples 1-2: Basic: 8–10, 14–18, 27 Average: 8–10, 14–18, 24, 27 Advanced: 8–10, 14–18, 24–27
☐ Examples 1-4: Basic: 8–18, 21, 23, 25, 26, 28–32, 37–45 Average: 8–19, 21, 22–31, 33, 36–44
  Advanced: 8–14, 19–44

REACHING ALL LEARNERS – Differentiated Instruction for students with

Developing Knowledge	On-level Knowledge	Advanced Knowledge	English Language Development
☐ Modeling TE p. 243	☐ Modeling TE p. 243	☐ Modeling TE p. 243	☐ Modeling TE p. 243
☐ Practice A 4-4 CRB	☐ Practice B 4-4 CRB	☐ Practice C 4-4 CRB	☐ Practice A, B, or C 4-4 CRB
☐ Reteach 4-4 CRB		☐ Challenge 4-4 CRB	☐ *Success for ELL* 4-4
☐ Homework Help Online Keyword: MR4 4-4	☐ Homework Help Online Keyword: MR4 4-4	☐ Homework Help Online Keyword: MR4 4-4	☐ Homework Help Online Keyword: MR4 4-4
☐ *Lesson Tutorial Video* 4-4	☐ *Lesson Tutorial Video* 4-4	☐ *Lesson Tutorial Video* 4-4	☐ *Lesson Tutorial Video* 4-4
☐ Reading Strategies 4-4 CRB	☐ Problem Solving 4-4 CRB	☐ Problem Solving 4-4 CRB	☐ Reading Strategies 4-4 CRB
☐ Questioning Strategies TE p. 243, 244	☐ Algebra TE p. 247	☐ Critical Thinking TE p. 245	☐ Vocabulary Exercises SE p. 242
☐ *IDEA Works!* 4-4			☐ *Multilingual Glossary*

ASSESSMENT
☐ Lesson Quiz, TE p. 249 and Transparency 4-4
☐ State-Specific Test Prep Online Keyword: MR4 TestPrep

Holt Geometry

Lesson Plan 4-5
Triangle Congruence: ASA, AAS, and HL pp. 252–259   Day _____

Objectives Apply ASA, AAS, and HL to construct triangles and to solve problems. Prove triangles congruent by using ASA, AAS, and HL.

> **NCTM Standards:** students should analyze characteristics and properties of two-and three-dimensional geometric shapes and develop mathematical arguments about geometric relationships.

Pacing
☐ 45-minute Classes: 1 day   ☐ 90-minute Classes: 1/2 day   ☐ Other_____

WARM UP
☐ Warm Up TE p. 252 and Warm Up Transparency 4-5
☐ Countdown to Testing Transparency, Week 8

TEACH
☐ Lesson Presentation CD-ROM 4-5
☐ Alternate Opener, Exploration Transparency 4-5, TE p. 252
☐ Reaching All Learners TE p. 253
☐ Additional Examples Transparencies 4-5
☐ Teaching Transparency 4-5
☐ *Know-It Notebook* 4-5

PRACTICE AND APPLY
☐ Examples 1-2: Basic: 9–12, 17, 25 Average: 9–12, 17, 21, 25 Advanced: 9–12, 17, 21, 25, 32
☐ Examples 1-4: Basic: 9–17, 19, 20, 22, 25, 26–30, 35–39 Average: 9–20, 22, 24–30, 34, 35–39
    Advanced: 9–16, 18, 19, 21–39

REACHING ALL LEARNERS – Differentiated Instruction for students with

Developing Knowledge	On-level Knowledge	Advanced Knowledge	English Language Development
☐ Inclusion TE p. 253, 255	☐ Auditory Cues TE p. 253	☐ Auditory Cues TE p. 253	☐ Auditory Cues TE p. 253
☐ Practice A 4-5 CRB	☐ Practice B 4-5 CRB	☐ Practice C 4-5 CRB	☐ Practice A, B, or C 4-5 CRB
☐ Reteach 4-5 CRB		☐ Challenge 4-5 CRB	☐ *Success for ELL* 4-5
☐ Homework Help Online Keyword: MR4 4-5	☐ Homework Help Online Keyword: MR4 4-5	☐ Homework Help Online Keyword: MR4 4-5	☐ Homework Help Online Keyword: MR4 4-5
☐ *Lesson Tutorial Video* 4-5	☐ *Lesson Tutorial Video* 4-5	☐ *Lesson Tutorial Video* 4-5	☐ *Lesson Tutorial Video* 4-5
☐ Reading Strategies 4-5 CRB	☐ Problem Solving 4-5 CRB	☐ Problem Solving 4-5 CRB	☐ Reading Strategies 4-5 CRB
☐ Questioning Strategies TE p. 253, 254, 255	☐ Reading Math TE p. 253	☐ Visual TE p. 255	☐ Vocabulary Exercises SE p. 252
☐ *IDEA Works!* 4-5			☐ *Multilingual Glossary*

ASSESSMENT
☐ Lesson Quiz, TE p. 259 and Transparency 4-5
☐ State-Specific Test Prep Online Keyword: MR4 TestPrep

Holt Geometry

Lesson Plan 4-6

Triangle Congruence: CPCTC pp. 260–265   *Day _____*

Objective Use CPCTC to prove parts of triangles are congruent.

NCTM Standards: students should analyze characteristics and properties of two-and three-dimensional geometric shapes and develop mathematical arguments about geometric relationships.

Pacing
☐ 45-minute Classes: 1 day   ☐ 90-minute Classes: 1/2 day   ☐ Other_____

WARM UP
☐ Warm Up TE p. 260 and Warm Up Transparency 4-6
☐ Countdown to Testing Transparency, Week 8

TEACH
☐ Lesson Presentation CD-ROM 4-6
☐ Alternate Opener, Exploration Transparency 4-6, TE p. 260
☐ Additional Examples Transparencies 4-6
☐ *Know-It Notebook* 4-6

PRACTICE AND APPLY
☐ Examples 1-2: Basic: 7–9, 17–19 Average: 7–9, 17–20 Advanced: 7–9, 17–20, 29, 32
☐ Examples 1-4: Basic: 7–19, 24–28, 33–37 Average: 7–16, 20–28, 30, 33–37 Advanced: 7–16, 19–37

REACHING ALL LEARNERS – Differentiated Instruction for students with

Developing Knowledge	On-level Knowledge	Advanced Knowledge	English Language Development
☐ Practice A 4-6 CRB	☐ Practice B 4-6 CRB	☐ Practice C 4-6 CRB	☐ Practice A, B, or C 4-6 CRB
☐ Reteach 4-6 CRB		☐ Challenge 4-6 CRB	☐ *Success for ELL* 4-6
☐ Homework Help Online Keyword: MR4 4-6	☐ Homework Help Online Keyword: MR4 4-6	☐ Homework Help Online Keyword: MR4 4-6	☐ Homework Help Online Keyword: MR4 4-6
☐ *Lesson Tutorial Video* 4-6	☐ *Lesson Tutorial Video* 4-6	☐ *Lesson Tutorial Video* 4-6	☐ *Lesson Tutorial Video* 4-6
☐ Reading Strategies 4-6 CRB	☐ Problem Solving 4-6 CRB	☐ Problem Solving 4-6 CRB	☐ Reading Strategies 4-6 CRB
☐ Questioning Strategies TE p. 261	☐ Auditory TE p. 261	☐ Critical Thinking TE p. 262	☐ Vocabulary Exercises SE p. 260
☐ *IDEA Works!* 4-6			☐ *Multilingual Glossary*

ASSESSMENT
☐ Lesson Quiz, TE p. 265 and Transparency 4-6
☐ State-Specific Test Prep Online Keyword: MR4 TestPrep

Holt Geometry

Teacher's Name _____ Class _____ Date _____

Lesson Plan 4-7
Introduction to Coordinate Proof pp. 267–272   *Day* _____

Objectives Position figures in the coordinate plane for use in coordinate proofs. Prove geometric concepts by using coordinate proof.

> **NCTM Standards:** students should use visualization, spatial reasoning, and geometric modeling to solve problems.

Pacing
☐ 45-minute Classes: 1 day   ☐ 90-minute Classes: 1/2 day   ☐ Other_____

WARM UP
☐ Warm Up TE p. 267 and Warm Up Transparency 4-7
☐ Countdown to Testing Transparency, Week 9

TEACH
☐ Lesson Presentation CD-ROM 4-7
☐ Alternate Opener, Exploration Transparency 4-7, TE p. 267
☐ Reaching All Learners TE p. 268
☐ Additional Examples Transparencies 4-7
☐ *Know-It Notebook* 4-7

PRACTICE AND APPLY
☐ Examples 1-2: Basic: 8–10, 15–17, 21 Average: 8–10, 15–17, 20–22 Advanced: 8–10, 15–17, 20–24
☐ Examples 1-4: Basic: 8–13, 15–21, 26–30, 35–40 Average: 8–15, 21, 22, 25–32, 35–40 Advanced: 8–15, 21–40

REACHING ALL LEARNERS – Differentiated Instruction for students with

Developing Knowledge	On-level Knowledge	Advanced Knowledge	English Language Development
☐ Inclusion TE p. 269	☐ Multiple Representations TE p. 268	☐ Multiple Representations TE p. 268	☐ Multiple Representations TE p. 268
☐ Practice A 4-7 CRB	☐ Practice B 4-7 CRB	☐ Practice C 4-7 CRB	☐ Practice A, B, or C 4-7 CRB
☐ Reteach 4-7 CRB		☐ Challenge 4-7 CRB	☐ *Success for ELL* 4-7
☐ Homework Help Online Keyword: MR4 4-7	☐ Homework Help Online Keyword: MR4 4-7	☐ Homework Help Online Keyword: MR4 4-7	☐ Homework Help Online Keyword: MR4 4-7
☐ *Lesson Tutorial Video* 4-7	☐ *Lesson Tutorial Video* 4-7	☐ *Lesson Tutorial Video* 4-7	☐ *Lesson Tutorial Video* 4-7
☐ Reading Strategies 4-7 CRB	☐ Problem Solving 4-7 CRB	☐ Problem Solving 4-7 CRB	☐ Reading Strategies 4-7 CRB
☐ Questioning Strategies TE p. 268, 269	☐ Social Studies TE p. 268	☐ Algebra TE p. 269	☐ Vocabulary Exercises SE p. 267
☐ *IDEA Works!* 4-7			☐ *Multilingual Glossary*

ASSESSMENT
☐ Lesson Quiz, TE p. 272 and Transparency 4-7
☐ State-Specific Test Prep Online Keyword: MR4 TestPrep

Holt Geometry

Lesson Plan 4-8
Isosceles and Equilateral Triangles pp. 273–279   Day _____

Objectives Prove theorems about isosceles and equilateral triangles. Apply properties of isosceles and equilateral triangles.

> **NCTM Standards:** students should understand numbers, ways of representing numbers, relationships among numbers, and number systems.

Pacing
☐ 45-minute Classes: 1 day   ☐ 90-minute Classes: 1/2 day   ☐ Other_____

WARM UP
☐ Warm Up TE p. 273 and Warm Up Transparency 4-8
☐ Countdown to Testing Transparency, Week 9

TEACH
☐ Lesson Presentation CD-ROM 4-8
☐ Alternate Opener, Exploration Transparency 4-8, TE p. 273
☐ Reaching All Learners TE p. 274
☐ Additional Examples Transparencies 4-8
☐ Teaching Transparency 4-8
☐ *Know-It Notebook* 4-8

PRACTICE AND APPLY
☐ Examples 1-2: Basic: 12–16, 22–25, 28, 29, 32–34 Average: 12–16, 22–25, 28, 29, 32–39 Advanced: 12–16, 22–25, 28, 29, 32–39, 41, 45
☐ Examples 1-4: Basic: 12–25, 28–30, 42–44, 48–54 Average: 12–23, 26–31, 33, 35, 36, 40, 42–44, 47–54 Advanced: 12–21, 26–33, 35–54

REACHING ALL LEARNERS – Differentiated Instruction for students with

Developing Knowledge	On-level Knowledge	Advanced Knowledge	English Language Development
☐ Visual Cues TE p. 274	☐ Visual Cues TE p. 274	☐ Visual Cues TE p. 274	☐ Visual Cues TE p. 274
☐ Practice A 4-8 CRB	☐ Practice B 4-8 CRB	☐ Practice C 4-8 CRB	☐ Practice A, B, or C 4-8 CRB
☐ Reteach 4-8 CRB		☐ Challenge 4-8 CRB	☐ *Success for ELL* 4-8
☐ Homework Help Online Keyword: MR4 4-8	☐ Homework Help Online Keyword: MR4 4-8	☐ Homework Help Online Keyword: MR4 4-8	☐ Homework Help Online Keyword: MR4 4-8
☐ *Lesson Tutorial Video* 4-8	☐ *Lesson Tutorial Video* 4-8	☐ *Lesson Tutorial Video* 4-8	☐ *Lesson Tutorial Video* 4-8
☐ Reading Strategies 4-8 CRB	☐ Problem Solving 4-8 CRB	☐ Problem Solving 4-8 CRB	☐ Reading Strategies 4-8 CRB
☐ Questioning Strategies TE p. 274, 275	☐ Multiple Representations TE p. 275	☐ Algebra TE p. 276	☐ Vocabulary Exercises SE p. 273
☐ *IDEA Works!* 4-8			☐ *Multilingual Glossary*

ASSESSMENT
☐ Lesson Quiz, TE p. 279 and Transparency 4-8
☐ State-Specific Test Prep Online Keyword: MR4 TestPrep

Holt Geometry

Teacher's Name _____ Class _____ Date _____

Lesson Plan 5-1
Perpendicular and Angle Bisectors pp. 300–306   Day _____

Objectives Prove and apply theorems about perpendicular bisectors. Prove and apply theorems about angle bisectors.

> **NCTM Standards:** students should understand meanings of operations and how they relate to one another.

Pacing
☐ 45-minute Classes: 1 day   ☐ 90-minute Classes: 1/2 day   ☐ Other_____

WARM UP
☐ Warm Up TE p. 300 and Warm Up Transparency 5-1
☐ Countdown to Testing Transparency, Week 10

TEACH
☐ Lesson Presentation CD-ROM 5-1
☐ Alternate Opener, Exploration Transparency 5-1, TE p. 300
☐ Reaching All Learners TE p. 217
☐ Additional Examples Transparencies 5-1
☐ Teaching Transparency 5-1
☐ *Know-It Notebook* 5-1

PRACTICE AND APPLY
☐ Examples 1-2: Basic: 12–17, 23–28 Average: 12–17, 22–29 Advanced: 12–17, 22–30, 39, 41
☐ Examples 1-4: Basic: 12–29, 33, 35–37, 42–48 Average: 12–29, 32–38, 42–48 Advanced: 12–21, 24–28 even, 29–48

REACHING ALL LEARNERS – Differentiated Instruction for students with

Developing Knowledge	On-level Knowledge	Advanced Knowledge	English Language Development
☐ Inclusion TE p. 303	☐ Concrete Manipulatives TE p. 301	☐ Concrete Manipulatives TE p. 301	☐ Concrete Manipulatives TE p. 301
☐ Practice A 5-1 CRB	☐ Practice B 5-1 CRB	☐ Practice C 5-1 CRB	☐ Practice A, B, or C 5-1 CRB
☐ Reteach 5-1 CRB		☐ Challenge 5-1 CRB	☐ *Success for ELL* 5-1
☐ Homework Help Online Keyword: MR4 5-1	☐ Homework Help Online Keyword: MR4 5-1	☐ Homework Help Online Keyword: MR4 5-1	☐ Homework Help Online Keyword: MR4 5-1
☐ *Lesson Tutorial Video* 5-1	☐ *Lesson Tutorial Video* 5-1	☐ *Lesson Tutorial Video* 5-1	☐ *Lesson Tutorial Video* 5-1
☐ Reading *Strategies* 5-1 CRB	☐ Problem Solving 5-1 CRB	☐ Problem Solving 5-1 CRB	☐ Reading *Strategies* 5-1 CRB
☐ Questioning Strategies TE p. 301, 302, 303	☐ Visual TE p. 301	☐ Critical Thinking TE p. 302	☐ Vocabulary Exercises SE p. 300
☐ *IDEA Works!* 5-1			☐ *Multilingual Glossary*

ASSESSMENT
☐ Lesson Quiz, TE p. 306 and Transparency 5-1
☐ State-Specific Test Prep Online Keyword: MR4 TestPrep

Holt Geometry

Lesson Plan 5-2
Bisectors of Triangles pp. 307–313   Day _____

Objectives Prove and apply properties of perpendicular bisectors of a triangle. Prove and apply
  properties of angle bisectors of a triangle.

> **NCTM Standards:** students should analyze characteristics and properties of two-and three-
>   dimensional geometric shapes and develop mathematical arguments about geometric relationships.

Pacing
☐ 45-minute Classes: 1 day   ☐ 90-minute Classes: 1/2 day   ☐ Other_____

WARM UP
☐ Warm Up TE p. 307 and Warm Up Transparency 5-2
☐ Countdown to Testing Transparency, Week 10

TEACH
☐ Lesson Presentation CD-ROM 5-2
☐ Alternate Opener, Exploration Transparency 5-2, TE p. 307
☐ Reaching All Learners TE p. 308
☐ Additional Examples Transparencies 5-2
☐ Teaching Transparency 5-2
☐ *Technology Lab Activities* 5-2
☐ *Know-It Notebook* 5-2

PRACTICE AND APPLY
☐ Examples 1-2: Basic: 12–17, 30, 32–34 Average: 12–17, 30, 32–34, 36, 43 Advanced: 12–17, 30,
  32–34, 29–31, 36, 43, 44
☐ Examples 1-4: Basic: 12–20, 22–35, 37, 40–42, 45–53 Average: 12–21, 22–28 even, 30–43, 45–53
  Advanced: 12–21, 22–28 even, 29–53

REACHING ALL LEARNERS – Differentiated Instruction for students with

Developing Knowledge	On-level Knowledge	Advanced Knowledge	English Language Development
☐ Multiple Representations TE p. 308	☐ Multiple Representations TE p. 308	☐ Multiple Representations TE p. 308	☐ Multiple Representations TE p. 308
☐ Practice A 5-2 CRB	☐ Practice B 5-2 CRB	☐ Practice C 5-2 CRB	☐ Practice A, B, or C 5-2 CRB
☐ Reteach 5-2 CRB		☐ Challenge 5-2 CRB	☐ *Success for ELL* 5-2
☐ Homework Help Online Keyword: MR4 5-2	☐ Homework Help Online Keyword: MR4 5-2	☐ Homework Help Online Keyword: MR4 5-2	☐ Homework Help Online Keyword: MR4 5-2
☐ *Lesson Tutorial Video* 5-2	☐ *Lesson Tutorial Video* 5-2	☐ *Lesson Tutorial Video* 5-2	☐ *Lesson Tutorial Video* 5-2
☐ Reading Strategies 5-2 CRB	☐ Problem Solving 5-2 CRB	☐ Problem Solving 5-2 CRB	☐ Reading Strategies 5-2 CRB
☐ Questioning Strategies TE p. 308, 309, 310	☐ Technology TE p. 309	☐ Algebra TE p. 312	☐ Vocabulary Exercises SE p. 307
☐ *IDEA Works!* 5-2			☐ *Multilingual Glossary*

ASSESSMENT
☐ Lesson Quiz, TE p. 313 and Transparency 5-2
☐ State-Specific Test Prep Online Keyword: MR4 TestPrep

Holt Geometry

Lesson Plan 5-3
Medians and Altitudes of Triangles pp. 314–320   Day _____

Objectives Apply properties of medians of a triangle. Apply properties of altitudes of a triangle.

NCTM Standards: students should understand numbers, ways of representing numbers, relationships among numbers, and number systems.

Pacing
☐ 45-minute Classes: 1 day   ☐ 90-minute Classes: 1/2 day   ☐ Other_____

WARM UP
☐ Warm Up TE p. 314 and Warm Up Transparency 5-3
☐ Countdown to Testing Transparency, Week 10

TEACH
☐ Lesson Presentation CD-ROM 5-3
☐ Alternate Opener, Exploration Transparency 5-3, TE p. 314
☐ Reaching All Learners TE p. 315
☐ Additional Examples Transparencies 5-3
☐ Teaching Transparency 5-3
☐ *Geometry Lab Activities* 5-3
☐ *Technology Lab Activities* 5-3
☐ *Know-It Notebook* 5-3

PRACTICE AND APPLY
☐ Examples 1-3: Basic: 12–32, 34–37, 40–43, 46–51 Average: 12–37, 39–43, 45–51 Advanced: 12–51

REACHING ALL LEARNERS – Differentiated Instruction for students with

Developing Knowledge	On-level Knowledge	Advanced Knowledge	English Language Development
☐ Inclusion TE p. 316	☐ Modeling TE p. 315	☐ Modeling TE p. 315	☐ Modeling TE p. 315
☐ Practice A 5-3 CRB	☐ Practice B 5-3 CRB	☐ Practice C 5-3 CRB	☐ Practice A, B, or C 5-3 CRB
☐ Reteach 5-3 CRB		☐ Challenge 5-3 CRB	☐ *Success for ELL* 5-3
☐ Homework Help Online Keyword: MR4 5-3	☐ Homework Help Online Keyword: MR4 5-3	☐ Homework Help Online Keyword: MR4 5-3	☐ Homework Help Online Keyword: MR4 5-3
☐ *Lesson Tutorial Video* 5-3	☐ *Lesson Tutorial Video* 5-3	☐ *Lesson Tutorial Video* 5-3	☐ *Lesson Tutorial Video* 5-3
☐ Reading Strategies 5-3 CRB	☐ Problem Solving 5-3 CRB	☐ Problem Solving 5-3 CRB	☐ Reading Strategies 5-3 CRB
☐ Questioning Strategies TE p. 315, 233	☐ Communicating Math TE p. 320	☐ Critical Thinking TE p. 316	☐ Vocabulary Exercises SE p. 314
☐ *IDEA Works!* 5-3			☐ *Multilingual Glossary*

ASSESSMENT
☐ Lesson Quiz, TE p. 320 and Transparency 5-3
☐ State-Specific Test Prep Online Keyword: MR4 TestPrep

Holt Geometry

Teacher's Name _____ Class _____ Date _____

Lesson Plan 5-4
The Triangle Midsegment Theorem pp. 322–327 Day _____

Objective Prove and use properties of triangle midsegments.

> **NCTM Standards:** students should compute fluently and make reasonable estimates.

Pacing
☐ 45-minute Classes: 1 day   ☐ 90-minute Classes: 1/2 day   ☐ Other_____

WARM UP
☐ Warm Up TE p. 322 and Warm Up Transparency 5-4
☐ Countdown to Testing Transparency, Week 11

TEACH
☐ Lesson Presentation CD-ROM 5-4
☐ Alternate Opener, Exploration Transparency 5-4, TE p. 322
☐ Additional Examples Transparencies 5-4
☐ Teaching Transparency 5-4
☐ *Know-It Notebook* 5-4

PRACTICE AND APPLY
☐ Examples 1-3: Basic: 10–27, 29–41, 48–55 Average: 10–44, 47–55 Advanced: 10–26, 28–55

REACHING ALL LEARNERS – Differentiated Instruction for students with

Developing Knowledge	On-level Knowledge	Advanced Knowledge	English Language Development
☐ Inclusion TE p. 323			
☐ Practice A 5-4 CRB	☐ Practice B 5-4 CRB	☐ Practice C 5-4 CRB	☐ Practice A, B, or C 5-4 CRB
☐ Reteach 5-4 CRB		☐ Challenge 5-4 CRB	☐ *Success for ELL* 5-4
☐ Homework Help Online Keyword: MR4 5-4	☐ Homework Help Online Keyword: MR4 5-4	☐ Homework Help Online Keyword: MR4 5-4	☐ Homework Help Online Keyword: MR4 5-4
☐ *Lesson Tutorial Video* 5-4	☐ *Lesson Tutorial Video* 5-4	☐ *Lesson Tutorial Video* 5-4	☐ *Lesson Tutorial Video* 5-4
☐ Reading Strategies 5-4 CRB	☐ Problem Solving 5-4 CRB	☐ Problem Solving 5-4 CRB	☐ Reading Strategies 5-4 CRB
☐ Questioning Strategies TE p. 323	☐ Kinesthetic TE p. 327	☐ Algebra TE p. 325	☐ Vocabulary Exercises SE p. 322
☐ *IDEA Works!* 5-4			☐ *Multilingual Glossary*

ASSESSMENT
☐ Lesson Quiz, TE p. 327 and Transparency 5-4
☐ State-Specific Test Prep Online Keyword: MR4 TestPrep

Holt Geometry

Teacher's Name _____ Class _____ Date _____

Lesson Plan 5-5

Indirect Proof and Inequalities in One Triangle pp. 332–339   Day _____

Objectives Write indirect proofs. Apply inequalities in one triangle.

NCTM Standards: students should develop and evaluate mathematical arguments and proofs.

Pacing
☐ 45-minute Classes: 1 day   ☐ 90-minute Classes: 1/2 day   ☐ Other_____

WARM UP
☐ Warm Up TE p. 332 and Warm Up Transparency 5-5
☐ Countdown to Testing Transparency, Week 11

TEACH
☐ Lesson Presentation CD-ROM 5-5
☐ Alternate Opener, Exploration Transparency 5-5, TE p. 332
☐ Reaching All Learners TE p. 333
☐ Additional Examples Transparencies 5-5
☐ Teaching Transparency 5-5
☐ *Know-It Notebook* 5-5

PRACTICE AND APPLY
☐ Examples 1-3: Basic: 16–25, 36–39, 42–57 Average: 16–25, 34, 36–57, 66, 67, 73 Advanced: 16–25, 34–57, 66–68, 73, 75
☐ Examples 1-5: Basic: 16–32, 36–39, 42–57, 59–65, 70–72, 76–81 Average: 16–34, 40–52, 54–73, 76–81 Advanced: 16–35, 40–52, 54–81

REACHING ALL LEARNERS – Differentiated Instruction for students with

Developing Knowledge	On-level Knowledge	Advanced Knowledge	English Language Development
☐ Visual Cues TE p. 333	☐ Visual Cues TE p. 333	☐ Visual Cues TE p. 333	☐ Visual Cues TE p. 333
☐ Practice A 5-5 CRB	☐ Practice B 5-5 CRB	☐ Practice C 5-5 CRB	☐ Practice A, B, or C 5-5 CRB
☐ Reteach 5-5 CRB		☐ Challenge 5-5 CRB	☐ *Success for ELL* 5-5
☐ Homework Help Online Keyword: MR4 5-5	☐ Homework Help Online Keyword: MR4 5-5	☐ Homework Help Online Keyword: MR4 5-5	☐ Homework Help Online Keyword: MR4 5-5
☐ *Lesson Tutorial Video* 5-5	☐ *Lesson Tutorial Video* 5-5	☐ *Lesson Tutorial Video* 5-5	☐ *Lesson Tutorial Video* 5-5
☐ Reading Strategies 5-5 CRB	☐ Problem Solving 5-5 CRB	☐ Problem Solving 5-5 CRB	☐ Reading Strategies 5-5 CRB
☐ Questioning Strategies TE p. 333, 334, 335	☐ Communicating Math TE p. 338	☐ Multiple Representations TE p. 338	☐ Vocabulary Exercises SE p. 332
☐ *IDEA Works!* 5-5			☐ *Multilingual Glossary*

ASSESSMENT
☐ Lesson Quiz, TE p. 339 and Transparency 5-5
☐ State-Specific Test Prep Online Keyword: MR4 TestPrep

Holt Geometry

Lesson Plan 5-6
Inequalities in Two Triangles pp. 340–345   Day _____

Objective Apply inequalities in two triangles.

> **NCTM Standards:** students should make and investigate mathematical conjectures.

Pacing
☐ 45-minute Classes: 1 day   ☐ 90-minute Classes: 1/2 day ☐ Other_____

WARM UP
☐ Warm Up TE p. 340 and Warm Up Transparency 5-6
☐ Countdown to Testing Transparency, Week 11

TEACH
☐ Lesson Presentation CD-ROM 5-6
☐ Alternate Opener, Exploration Transparency 5-6, TE p. 340
☐ Reaching All Learners TE p. 341
☐ Additional Examples Transparencies 5-6
☐ Teaching Transparency 5-6
☐ *Know-It Notebook* 5-6

PRACTICE AND APPLY
☐ Examples 1-3: Basic: 9–16, 18–28, 30–33, 36–43 Average: 9–34, 36–43 Advanced: 9–43

REACHING ALL LEARNERS – Differentiated Instruction for students with

Developing Knowledge	On-level Knowledge	Advanced Knowledge	English Language Development
☐ Kinesthetic Experience TE p. 341	☐ Kinesthetic Experience TE p. 341	☐ Kinesthetic Experience TE p. 341	☐ Kinesthetic Experience TE p. 341
☐ Practice A 5-6 CRB	☐ Practice B 5-6 CRB	☐ Practice C 5-6 CRB	☐ Practice A, B, or C 5-6 CRB
☐ Reteach 5-6 CRB		☐ Challenge 5-6 CRB	☐ *Success for ELL* 5-6
☐ Homework Help Online Keyword: MR4 5-6	☐ Homework Help Online Keyword: MR4 5-6	☐ Homework Help Online Keyword: MR4 5-6	☐ Homework Help Online Keyword: MR4 5-6
☐ *Lesson Tutorial Video* 5-6	☐ *Lesson Tutorial Video* 5-6	☐ *Lesson Tutorial Video* 5-6	☐ *Lesson Tutorial Video* 5-6
☐ Reading Strategies 5-6 CRB	☐ Problem Solving 5-6 CRB	☐ Problem Solving 5-6 CRB	☐ Reading Strategies 5-6 CRB
☐ Questioning Strategies TE p. 341, 342	☐ Kinesthetic TE p. 341	☐ Visual TE p. 342	☐ Reading Math TE p. 344
☐ *IDEA Works!* 5-6			☐ *Multilingual Glossary*

ASSESSMENT
☐ Lesson Quiz, TE p. 345 and Transparency 5-6
☐ State-Specific Test Prep Online Keyword: MR4 TestPrep

Holt Geometry

Teacher's Name _____ Class _____ Date _____

Lesson Plan 5-7
The Pythagorean Theorem pp. 348–355   Day _____

Objectives Use the Pythagorean Theorem and its converse to solve problems. Use Pythagorean inequalities to classify triangles.

NCTM Standards: students should use visualization, spatial reasoning, and geometric modeling to solve problems.

Pacing
☐ 45-minute Classes: 1 day   ☐ 90-minute Classes: 1/2 day   ☐ Other_____

WARM UP
☐ Warm Up TE p. 348 and Warm Up Transparency 5-7
☐ Countdown to Testing Transparency, Week 12

TEACH
☐ Lesson Presentation CD-ROM 5-7
☐ Alternate Opener, Exploration Transparency 5-7, TE p. 348
☐ Reaching All Learners TE p. 268
☐ Additional Examples Transparencies 5-7
☐ Teaching Transparency 5-7
☐ *Technology Lab Activities* 5-7
☐ *Know-It Notebook* 5-7

PRACTICE AND APPLY
☐ Examples 1-2: Basic: 15–18, 30–36, 38–40 Average: 15–18, 30–36, 38–43, 45, 46 Advanced: 15–18, 30–36, 38–43, 45, 46, 53, 54
☐ Examples 1-4: Basic: 15–36, 38–44, 47–51, 56–61 Average: 15–51, 55–61 Advanced: 15–28, 30–61

REACHING ALL LEARNERS – Differentiated Instruction for students with

Developing Knowledge	On-level Knowledge	Advanced Knowledge	English Language Development
☐ Inclusion TE p. 353	☐ Concrete Manipulatives TE p. 349	☐ Concrete Manipulatives TE p. 349	☐ Concrete Manipulatives TE p. 349
☐ Practice A 5-7 CRB	☐ Practice B 5-7 CRB	☐ Practice C 5-7 CRB	☐ Practice A, B, or C 5-7 CRB
☐ Reteach 5-7 CRB		☐ Challenge 5-7 CRB	☐ *Success for ELL* 5-7
☐ Homework Help Online Keyword: MR4 5-7	☐ Homework Help Online Keyword: MR4 5-7	☐ Homework Help Online Keyword: MR4 5-7	☐ Homework Help Online Keyword: MR4 5-7
☐ *Lesson Tutorial Video* 5-7	☐ *Lesson Tutorial Video* 5-7	☐ *Lesson Tutorial Video* 5-7	☐ *Lesson Tutorial Video* 5-7
☐ Reading Strategies 5-7 CRB	☐ Problem Solving 5-7 CRB	☐ Problem Solving 5-7 CRB	☐ Reading Strategies 5-7 CRB
☐ Questioning Strategies TE p. 349, 350, 351	☐ Critical Thinking TE p. 350	☐ Social Studies Link TE p. 350	☐ Vocabulary Exercises SE p. 348
☐ *IDEA Works!* 5-7			☐ *Multilingual Glossary*

ASSESSMENT
☐ Lesson Quiz, TE p. 355 and Transparency 5-7
☐ State-Specific Test Prep Online Keyword: MR4 TestPrep

Holt Geometry

Teacher's Name _____ Class _____ Date _____

Lesson Plan 5-8
Applying Special Right Triangles pp. 356–362   *Day* _____

Objectives Justify and apply properties of 45°-45°-90° triangles. Justify and apply properties of 30°-60°-90° triangles.

NCTM Standards: students should analyze change in various contexts.

Pacing
☐ 45-minute Classes: 1 day   ☐ 90-minute Classes: 1/2 day   ☐ Other_____

WARM UP
☐ Warm Up TE p. 356 and Warm Up Transparency 5-8
☐ Countdown to Testing Transparency, Week 12

TEACH
☐ Lesson Presentation CD-ROM 5-8
☐ Alternate Opener, Exploration Transparency 5-8, TE p. 356
☐ Reaching All Learners TE p. 357
☐ Additional Examples Transparencies 5-8
☐ Teaching Transparency 5-8
☐ *Geometry Lab Activities* 5-8
☐ *Know-It Notebook* 5-8

PRACTICE AND APPLY
☐ Examples 1-2: Basic: 9–12, 17, 19, 22 Average: 9–12, 17, 19, 22, 24, 25 Advanced: 9–12, 17, 19, 22, 24, 25, 34
☐ Examples 1-4: Basic: 9–22, 24–33, 38–46 Average: 9–35, 38–46 Advanced: 9–46

REACHING ALL LEARNERS – Differentiated Instruction for students with

Developing Knowledge	On-level Knowledge	Advanced Knowledge	English Language Development
☐ Inclusion TE p. 360	☐ Auditory Cues TE p. 357	☐ Auditory Cues TE p. 357	☐ Auditory Cues TE p. 357
☐ Practice A 5-8 CRB	☐ Practice B 5-8 CRB	☐ Practice C 5-8 CRB	☐ Practice A, B, or C 5-8 CRB
☐ Reteach 5-8 CRB		☐ Challenge 5-8 CRB	☐ *Success for ELL* 5-8
☐ Homework Help Online Keyword: MR4 5-8	☐ Homework Help Online Keyword: MR4 5-8	☐ Homework Help Online Keyword: MR4 5-8	☐ Homework Help Online Keyword: MR4 5-8
☐ *Lesson Tutorial Video* 5-8	☐ *Lesson Tutorial Video* 5-8	☐ *Lesson Tutorial Video* 5-8	☐ *Lesson Tutorial Video* 5-8
☐ Reading Strategies 5-8 CRB	☐ Problem Solving 5-8 CRB	☐ Problem Solving 5-8 CRB	☐ Reading Strategies 5-8 CRB
☐ Questioning Strategies TE p. 357, 358, 359	☐ Algebra TE p. 357	☐ Critical Thinking TE p. 358	
☐ *IDEA Works!* 5-8			☐ *Multilingual Glossary*

ASSESSMENT
☐ Lesson Quiz, TE p. 362 and Transparency 5-8
☐ State-Specific Test Prep Online Keyword: MR4 TestPrep

Holt Geometry

Teacher's Name _____ Class _____ Date _____

Lesson Plan 6-1
Properties and Attributes of Polygons pp. 382–388   *Day _____*

Objectives Classify polygons based on their sides and angles. Find and use the measures of interior
and exterior angles of polygons.

NCTM Standards: students should understand patterns, relations, and functions.

Pacing
☐ 45-minute Classes: 1 day   ☐ 90-minute Classes: 1/2 day   ☐ Other_____

WARM UP
☐ Warm Up TE p. 382 and Warm Up Transparency 6-1
☐ Countdown to Testing Transparency, Week 13

TEACH
☐ Lesson Presentation CD-ROM 6-1
☐ Alternate Opener, Exploration Transparency 6-1, TE p. 382
☐ Reaching All Learners TE p. 383
☐ Additional Examples Transparencies 6-1
☐ Teaching Transparency 6-1
☐ *Know-It Notebook* 6-1

PRACTICE AND APPLY
☐ Examples 1-3: Basic: 16–24, 29, 30, 35–38, 46–50 Average: 16–24, 29, 30, 35–38, 44, 46–50
    Advanced: 16–24, 29, 30, 35–38, 44, 46–50, 56, 57
☐ Examples 1-5: Basic: 16–31, 32–42 even, 43, 45–50, 53–55, 60–67 Average: 16–46, 51–56, 60–67
    Advanced: 16–42, 44, 45, 51–67

REACHING ALL LEARNERS – Differentiated Instruction for students with

Developing Knowledge	On-level Knowledge	Advanced Knowledge	English Language Development
☐ Inclusion TE p. 384	☐ Concrete Manipulatives TE p. 383	☐ Concrete Manipulatives TE p. 383	☐ Concrete Manipulatives TE p. 383
☐ Practice A 6-1 CRB	☐ Practice B 6-1 CRB	☐ Practice C 6-1 CRB	☐ Practice A, B, or C 6-1 CRB
☐ Reteach 6-1 CRB		☐ Challenge 6-1 CRB	☐ *Success for ELL* 6-1
☐ Homework Help Online Keyword: MR4 6-1	☐ Homework Help Online Keyword: MR4 6-1	☐ Homework Help Online Keyword: MR4 6-1	☐ Homework Help Online Keyword: MR4 6-1
☐ *Lesson Tutorial Video* 6-1	☐ *Lesson Tutorial Video* 6-1	☐ *Lesson Tutorial Video* 6-1	☐ *Lesson Tutorial Video* 6-1
☐ Reading *Strategies* 6-1 CRB	☐ Problem Solving 6-1 CRB	☐ Problem Solving 6-1 CRB	☐ Reading *Strategies* 6-1 CRB
☐ Questioning Strategies TE p. 383, 384, 385	☐ Algebra TE p. 383	☐ Critical Thinking TE p. 383	☐ Vocabulary Exercises SE p. 382
☐ *IDEA Works!* 6-1			☐ *Multilingual Glossary*

ASSESSMENT
☐ Lesson Quiz, TE p. 388 and Transparency 6-1
☐ State-Specific Test Prep Online Keyword: MR4 TestPrep

Holt Geometry

Lesson Plan 6-2
Properties of Parallelograms pp. 391–397   Day _____

Objectives Find the measures of interior and exterior angles of triangles. Apply theorems about the interior and exterior angles of triangles.

NCTM Standards: students should formulate questions that can be addressed with data and collect, organize, and display relevant data to answer them.

Pacing
☐ 45-minute Classes: 1 day   ☐ 90-minute Classes: 1/2 day ☐ Other_____

WARM UP
☐ Warm Up TE p. 391 and Warm Up Transparency 6-2
☐ Countdown to Testing Transparency, Week 13

TEACH
☐ Lesson Presentation CD-ROM 6-2
☐ Alternate Opener, Exploration Transparency 6-2, TE p. 391
☐ Reaching All Learners TE p. 392
☐ Additional Examples Transparencies 6-2
☐ Teaching Transparency 6-2
☐ *Technology Lab Activities* 6-2
☐ *Know-It Notebook* 6-2

PRACTICE AND APPLY
☐ Examples 1-2: Basic: 15–24, 27–30, 32–42 even Average: 15–24, 27–31, 32–40 even, 41–43, 46, 47
    Advanced: 15–24, 27–31, 32–40 even, 41–43, 46, 47, 56
☐ Examples 1-4: Basic: 15–30, 32–40, 42, 46, 48, 51–53, 58–66 Average: 15–26, 29, 30, 32–40 even,
    41–54, 58–66 Advanced: 15–31, 32–42 even, 44–66

REACHING ALL LEARNERS – Differentiated Instruction for students with

Developing Knowledge	On-level Knowledge	Advanced Knowledge	English Language Development
☐ Visual Cues TE p. 392	☐ Visual Cues TE p. 392	☐ Visual Cues TE p. 392	☐ Visual Cues TE p. 392
☐ Practice A 6-2 CRB	☐ Practice B 6-2 CRB	☐ Practice C 6-2 CRB	☐ Practice A, B, or C 6-2 CRB
☐ Reteach 6-2 CRB		☐ Challenge 6-2 CRB	☐ *Success for ELL* 6-2
☐ Homework Help Online Keyword: MR4 6-2	☐ Homework Help Online Keyword: MR4 6-2	☐ Homework Help Online Keyword: MR4 6-2	☐ Homework Help Online Keyword: MR4 6-2
☐ *Lesson Tutorial Video* 6-2	☐ *Lesson Tutorial Video* 6-2	☐ *Lesson Tutorial Video* 6-2	☐ *Lesson Tutorial Video* 6-2
☐ Reading Strategies 6-2 CRB	☐ Problem Solving 6-2 CRB	☐ Problem Solving 6-2 CRB	☐ Reading Strategies 6-2 CRB
☐ Questioning Strategies TE p. 392, 393, 394	☐ Visual TE p. 396	☐ Critical Thinking TE p. 395	☐ Vocabulary Exercises SE p. 391
☐ *IDEA Works!* 6-2			☐ *Multilingual Glossary*

ASSESSMENT
☐ Lesson Quiz, TE p. 397 and Transparency 6-2
☐ State-Specific Test Prep Online Keyword: MR4 TestPrep

Holt Geometry

Lesson Plan 6-3
Conditions for Parallelograms pp. 398–405 Day _____

Objective Prove that a given quadrilateral is a parallelogram.

> **NCTM Standards:** students should formulate questions that can be addressed with data and collect, organize, and display relevant data to answer them.

Pacing
☐ 45-minute Classes: 1 day   ☐ 90-minute Classes: 1/2 day   ☐ Other_____

WARM UP
☐ Warm Up TE p. 398 and Warm Up Transparency 6-3
☐ Countdown to Testing Transparency, Week 13

TEACH
☐ Lesson Presentation CD-ROM 6-3
☐ Alternate Opener, Exploration Transparency 6-3, TE p. 398
☐ Reaching All Learners TE p. 399
☐ Additional Examples Transparencies 6-3
☐ Teaching Transparency 6-3
☐ *Geometry Lab Activities* 6-3
☐ *Know-It Notebook* 6-3

PRACTICE AND APPLY
☐ Examples 1-2: Basic: 9–13, 17–20, 26, 27 Average: 9–13, 17–23, 26, 29 Advanced: 9–13, 17–23, 25–27, 29, 30, 33, 40
☐ Examples 1-4: Basic: 9–20, 26, 27, 34–37, 41–49 Average: 9–23, 24–32 even, 33–38, 41–49 Advanced: 9–16, 18, 20–49

REACHING ALL LEARNERS – Differentiated Instruction for students with

Developing Knowledge	On-level Knowledge	Advanced Knowledge	English Language Development
☐ Kinesthetic Experience TE p. 399	☐ Kinesthetic Experience TE p. 399	☐ Kinesthetic Experience TE p. 399	☐ Kinesthetic Experience TE p. 399
☐ Practice A 6-3 CRB	☐ Practice B 6-3 CRB	☐ Practice C 6-3 CRB	☐ Practice A, B, or C 6-3 CRB
☐ Reteach 6-3 CRB		☐ Challenge 6-3 CRB	☐ *Success for ELL* 6-3
☐ Homework Help Online Keyword: MR4 6-3	☐ Homework Help Online Keyword: MR4 6-3	☐ Homework Help Online Keyword: MR4 6-3	☐ Homework Help Online Keyword: MR4 6-3
☐ *Lesson Tutorial Video* 6-3	☐ *Lesson Tutorial Video* 6-3	☐ *Lesson Tutorial Video* 6-3	☐ *Lesson Tutorial Video* 6-3
☐ Reading Strategies 6-3 CRB	☐ Problem Solving 6-3 CRB	☐ Problem Solving 6-3 CRB	☐ Reading Strategies 6-3 CRB
☐ Questioning Strategies TE p. 399, 400, 401	☐ Reading Math TE p. 399	☐ Auditory TE p. 403	
☐ *IDEA Works!* 6-3			☐ *Multilingual Glossary*

ASSESSMENT
☐ Lesson Quiz, TE p. 405 and Transparency 6-3
☐ State-Specific Test Prep Online Keyword: MR4 TestPrep

Holt Geometry

Lesson Plan 6-4

Properties of Special Parallelograms pp. 408–415   Day _____

Objectives Prove and apply properties of rectangles, rhombuses, and squares. Use properties of rectangles, rhombuses, and squares to solve problems.

NCTM Standards: students should apply appropriate techniques, tools, and formulas to determine measurements.

Pacing
☐ 45-minute Classes: 1 day   ☐ 90-minute Classes: 1/2 day   ☐ Other_____

WARM UP
☐ Warm Up TE p. 408 and Warm Up Transparency 6-4
☐ Countdown to Testing Transparency, Week 14

TEACH
☐ Lesson Presentation CD-ROM 6-4
☐ Alternate Opener, Exploration Transparency 6-4, TE p. 408
☐ Reaching All Learners TE p. 409
☐ Additional Examples Transparencies 6-4
☐ Teaching Transparency 6-4
☐ *Geometry Lab Activities* 6-4
☐ *Know-It Notebook* 6-4

PRACTICE AND APPLY
☐ Examples 1-2: Basic: 10–15, 18–21, 24–30 even, 40–42 Average: 10–15, 18–30 even, 40–42, 51
   Advanced: 10–15, 18–30 even, 33, 40–42, 48, 51
☐ Examples 1-4: Basic: 10–23, 24–28 even, 29, 31, 34–36, 40–42, 44–47, 52–56 Average: 10–28,
   34–36, 39–48, 51–56 Advanced: 10–19, 22–32 even, 33, 35–56

REACHING ALL LEARNERS – Differentiated Instruction for students with

Developing Knowledge	On-level Knowledge	Advanced Knowledge	English Language Development
☐ Modeling TE p. 409	☐ Modeling TE p. 409	☐ Modeling TE p. 409	☐ Modeling TE p. 409
☐ Practice A 6-4 CRB	☐ Practice B 6-4 CRB	☐ Practice C 6-4 CRB	☐ Practice A, B, or C 6-4 CRB
☐ Reteach 6-4 CRB		☐ Challenge 6-4 CRB	☐ *Success for ELL* 6-4
☐ Homework Help Online Keyword: MR4 6-4	☐ Homework Help Online Keyword: MR4 6-4	☐ Homework Help Online Keyword: MR4 6-4	☐ Homework Help Online Keyword: MR4 6-4
☐ *Lesson Tutorial Video* 6-4	☐ *Lesson Tutorial Video* 6-4	☐ *Lesson Tutorial Video* 6-4	☐ *Lesson Tutorial Video* 6-4
☐ Reading Strategies 6-4 CRB	☐ Problem Solving 6-4 CRB	☐ Problem Solving 6-4 CRB	☐ Reading Strategies 6-4 CRB
☐ Questioning Strategies TE p. 409, 410, 411	☐ Reading Math TE p. 408	☐ Social Studies Link TE p. 413	☐ Vocabulary Exercises SE p. 408
☐ *IDEA Works!* 6-4			☐ *Multilingual Glossary*

ASSESSMENT
☐ Lesson Quiz, TE p. 415 and Transparency 6-4
☐ State-Specific Test Prep Online Keyword: MR4 TestPrep

Holt Geometry

Lesson Plan 6-5

Conditions for Special Parallelograms pp. 418–425   *Day* _____

Objective Prove that a given quadrilateral is a rectangle, rhombus, or square.

NCTM Standards: students should apply appropriate techniques, tools, and formulas to determine measurements.

Pacing
☐ 45-minute Classes: 1 day   ☐ 90-minute Classes: 1/2 day   ☐ Other_____

WARM UP
☐ Warm Up TE p. 418 and Warm Up Transparency 6-5
☐ Countdown to Testing Transparency, Week 14

TEACH
☐ Lesson Presentation CD-ROM 6-5
☐ Alternate Opener, Exploration Transparency 6-5, TE p. 418
☐ Reaching All Learners TE p. 419
☐ Additional Examples Transparencies 6-5
☐ Teaching Transparency 6-5
☐ *Know-It Notebook* 6-5

PRACTICE AND APPLY
☐ Examples 1-3: Basic: 6–17, 19, 20, 22, 28–30, 33, 35, 39–41, 45–52 Average: 6–10, 12–16 even, 17, 18, 20–24, 26–29, 31, 33, 35–41, 44–52 Advanced: 6–10, 12–24 even, 25–27, 29–52

REACHING ALL LEARNERS – Differentiated Instruction for students with

Developing Knowledge	On-level Knowledge	Advanced Knowledge	English Language Development
☐ Communication TE p. 419	☐ Communication TE p. 419	☐ Communication TE p. 419	☐ Communication TE p. 419
☐ Practice A 6-5 CRB	☐ Practice B 6-5 CRB	☐ Practice C 6-5 CRB	☐ Practice A, B, or C 6-5 CRB
☐ Reteach 6-5 CRB		☐ Challenge 6-5 CRB	☐ *Success for ELL* 6-5
☐ Homework Help Online Keyword: MR4 6-5	☐ Homework Help Online Keyword: MR4 6-5	☐ Homework Help Online Keyword: MR4 6-5	☐ Homework Help Online Keyword: MR4 6-5
☐ *Lesson Tutorial Video* 6-5	☐ *Lesson Tutorial Video* 6-5	☐ *Lesson Tutorial Video* 6-5	☐ *Lesson Tutorial Video* 6-5
☐ Reading Strategies 6-5 CRB	☐ Problem Solving 6-5 CRB	☐ Problem Solving 6-5 CRB	☐ Reading Strategies 6-5 CRB
☐ Questioning Strategies TE p. 419, 420	☐ Critical Thinking TE p. 419, 420	☐ Communicating Math TE p. 423	
☐ *IDEA Works!* 6-5			☐ *Multilingual Glossary*

ASSESSMENT
☐ Lesson Quiz, TE p. 425 and Transparency 6-5
☐ State-Specific Test Prep Online Keyword: MR4 TestPrep

Holt Geometry

Teacher's Name _____ Class _____ Date _____

Lesson Plan 6-6
Properties of Kites and Trapezoids pp. 427–435   Day _____

Objectives Use properties of kites to solve problems. Use properties of trapezoids to solve problems.

NCTM Standards: students should understand patterns, relations, and functions.

Pacing
☐ 45-minute Classes: 1 day   ☐ 90-minute Classes: 1/2 day ☐ Other_____

WARM UP
☐ Warm Up TE p. 427 and Warm Up Transparency 6-6
☐ Countdown to Testing Transparency, Week 14

TEACH
☐ Lesson Presentation CD-ROM 6-6
☐ Alternate Opener, Exploration Transparency 6-6, TE p. 427
☐ Reaching All Learners TE p. 428
☐ Additional Examples Transparencies 6-6
☐ Teaching Transparency 6-6
☐ *Geometry Lab Activities* 6-6
☐ *Technology Lab Activities* 6-6
☐ *Know-It Notebook* 6-6

PRACTICE AND APPLY
☐ Examples 1-2: Basic: 13–16, 24, 25, 28, 29, 31 Average: 13–16, 24, 25, 28, 29, 31, 37, 38 Advanced: 13–16, 24, 25, 28, 29, 31, 37–39
☐ Examples 1-5: Basic: 13–34, 40–42, 45, 47–49, 52–56 Average: 13–23, 24–32 even, 33–36, 38–42 even, 43–45, 47–49, 52–56 Advanced: 13–23, 28–32 even, 33, 35–42, 44–56

REACHING ALL LEARNERS – Differentiated Instruction for students with

Developing Knowledge	On-level Knowledge	Advanced Knowledge	English Language Development
☐ Multiple Representations TE p. 428	☐ Multiple Representations TE p. 428	☐ Multiple Representations TE p. 428	☐ Multiple Representations TE p. 428
☐ Practice A 6-6 CRB	☐ Practice B 6-6 CRB	☐ Practice C 6-6 CRB	☐ Practice A, B, or C 6-6 CRB
☐ Reteach 6-6 CRB		☐ Challenge 6-6 CRB	☐ *Success for ELL* 6-6
☐ Homework Help Online Keyword: MR4 6-6	☐ Homework Help Online Keyword: MR4 6-6	☐ Homework Help Online Keyword: MR4 6-6	☐ Homework Help Online Keyword: MR4 6-6
☐ *Lesson Tutorial Video* 6-6	☐ *Lesson Tutorial Video* 6-6	☐ *Lesson Tutorial Video* 6-6	☐ *Lesson Tutorial Video* 6-6
☐ Reading Strategies 6-6 CRB	☐ Problem Solving 6-6 CRB	☐ Problem Solving 6-6 CRB	☐ Reading Strategies 6-6 CRB
☐ Questioning Strategies TE p. 428, 429, 430, 431	☐ Algebra TE p. 430	☐ Critical Thinking TE p. 431	☐ Vocabulary Exercises SE p. 427
☐ *IDEA Works!* 6-6			☐ *Multilingual Glossary*

ASSESSMENT
☐ Lesson Quiz, TE p. 435 and Transparency 6-6
☐ State-Specific Test Prep Online Keyword: MR4 TestPrep

Holt Geometry

Teacher's Name _____ Class _____ Date _____

Lesson Plan 7-1

Ratio and Proportion pp. 454–459   *Day _____*

Objectives Write and simplify ratios. Use proportions to solve problems.

> **NCTM Standards:** students should use mathematical models to represent and understand quantitative relationships.

Pacing
☐ 45-minute Classes: 1 day   ☐ 90-minute Classes: 1/2 day   ☐ Other_____

WARM UP
☐ Warm Up TE p. 454 and Warm Up Transparency 7-1
☐ Countdown to Testing Transparency, Week 15

TEACH
☐ Lesson Presentation CD-ROM 7-1
☐ Alternate Opener, Exploration Transparency 7-1, TE p. 454
☐ Reaching All Learners TE p. 455
☐ Additional Examples Transparencies 7-1
☐ Teaching Transparency 7-1
☐ *Know-It Notebook* 7-1

PRACTICE AND APPLY
☐ Examples 1-3: Basic: 17–27, 34–38 Average: 17–27, 34–38, 40, 47 Advanced: 17–27, 34–37, 41, 51
☐ Examples 1-5: Basic: 17–32, 35–40, 42–47, 52–59 Average: 17–30, 32–36, 39–48, 51–59 Advanced: 17–33, 37–59

REACHING ALL LEARNERS – Differentiated Instruction for students with

Developing Knowledge	On-level Knowledge	Advanced Knowledge	English Language Development
☐ Inclusion TE p. 456	☐ Kinesthetic Experience TE p. 455	☐ Kinesthetic Experience TE p. 455	☐ Kinesthetic Experience TE p. 455
☐ Practice A 7-1 CRB	☐ Practice B 7-1 CRB	☐ Practice C 7-1 CRB	☐ Practice A, B, or C 7-1 CRB
☐ Reteach 7-1 CRB		☐ Challenge 7-1 CRB	☐ *Success for ELL* 7-1
☐ Homework Help Online Keyword: MR4 7-1	☐ Homework Help Online Keyword: MR4 7-1	☐ Homework Help Online Keyword: MR4 7-1	☐ Homework Help Online Keyword: MR4 7-1
☐ *Lesson Tutorial Video* 7-1	☐ *Lesson Tutorial Video* 7-1	☐ *Lesson Tutorial Video* 7-1	☐ *Lesson Tutorial Video* 7-1
☐ Reading *Strategies* 7-1 CRB	☐ Problem Solving 7-1 CRB	☐ Problem Solving 7-1 CRB	☐ Reading *Strategies* 7-1 CRB
☐ Questioning Strategies TE p. 455, 456	☐ Visual TE p. 458	☐ Algebra TE p. 455, 458	☐ Vocabulary Exercises SE p. 454
☐ *IDEA Works!* 7-1			☐ *Multilingual Glossary*

ASSESSMENT
☐ Lesson Quiz, TE p. 459 and Transparency 7-1
☐ State-Specific Test Prep Online Keyword: MR4 TestPrep

Holt Geometry

Lesson Plan 7-2

Ratios in Similar Polygons pp. 462–467   Day _____

Objectives Identify similar polygons. Apply properties of similar polygons to solve problems.

NCTM Standards: students should understand patterns, relations, and functions.

Pacing

☐ 45-minute Classes: 1 day   ☐ 90-minute Classes: 1/2 day ☐ Other_____

WARM UP

☐ Warm Up TE p. 462 and Warm Up Transparency 7-2
☐ Countdown to Testing Transparency, Week 15

TEACH

☐ Lesson Presentation CD-ROM 7-2
☐ Alternate Opener, Exploration Transparency 7-2, TE p. 462
☐ Reaching All Learners TE p. 463
☐ Additional Examples Transparencies 7-2
☐ Teaching Transparency 7-2
☐ *Geometry Lab Activities* 7-2
☐ *Know-It Notebook* 7-2

PRACTICE AND APPLY

☐ Examples 1-3: Basic: 7–17, 19–21, 25–29, 34–40 Average: 7–15, 18–20, 22–30, 34–40 Advanced:
   7–11, 12–20 even, 21–40

REACHING ALL LEARNERS – Differentiated Instruction for students with

Developing Knowledge	On-level Knowledge	Advanced Knowledge	English Language Development
☐ Inclusion TE p. 463	☐ Concrete Manipulatives TE p. 463	☐ Concrete Manipulatives TE p. 463	☐ Concrete Manipulatives TE p. 463
☐ Practice A 7-2 CRB	☐ Practice B 7-2 CRB	☐ Practice C 7-2 CRB	☐ Practice A, B, or C 7-2 CRB
☐ Reteach 7-2 CRB		☐ Challenge 7-2 CRB	☐ *Success for ELL* 7-2
☐ Homework Help Online Keyword: MR4 7-2	☐ Homework Help Online Keyword: MR4 7-2	☐ Homework Help Online Keyword: MR4 7-2	☐ Homework Help Online Keyword: MR4 7-2
☐ *Lesson Tutorial Video* 7-2	☐ *Lesson Tutorial Video* 7-2	☐ *Lesson Tutorial Video* 7-2	☐ *Lesson Tutorial Video* 7-2
☐ Reading Strategies 7-2 CRB	☐ Problem Solving 7-2 CRB	☐ Problem Solving 7-2 CRB	☐ Reading Strategies 7-2 CRB
☐ Questioning Strategies TE p. 463, 464	☐ Reading Math TE p. 464	☐ Visual TE p. 465	☐ Vocabulary Exercises SE p. 462
☐ *IDEA Works!* 7-2			☐ *Multilingual Glossary*

ASSESSMENT

☐ Lesson Quiz, TE p. 467 and Transparency 7-2
☐ State-Specific Test Prep Online Keyword: MR4 TestPrep

Holt Geometry

Teacher's Name _____ Class _____ Date _____

Lesson Plan 7-3
Triangle Similarity: AA, SSS, and SAS pp. 470–477   Day _____

Objectives Prove certain triangles are similar by using AA, SSS, and SAS. Use triangle similarity to solve problems.

> **NCTM Standards:** students should apply appropriate techniques, tools, and formulas to determine measurements.

Pacing
☐ 45-minute Classes: 1 day   ☐ 90-minute Classes: 1/2 day ☐ Other_____

WARM UP
☐ Warm Up TE p. 479 and Warm Up Transparency 7-3
☐ Countdown to Testing Transparency, Week 15

TEACH
☐ Lesson Presentation CD-ROM 7-3
☐ Alternate Opener, Exploration Transparency 7-3, TE p. 470
☐ Reaching All Learners TE p. 471
☐ Additional Examples Transparencies 7-3
☐ Teaching Transparency 7-3
☐ *Know-It Notebook* 7-3

PRACTICE AND APPLY
☐ Examples 1-3: Basic: 11–16, 20–24, 31 Average: 11–16, 19–24, 27, 31 Advanced: 11–16, 20–24, 27, 31, 37, 40
☐ Examples 1-5: Basic: 11–19, 23–25, 32–37, 41–46 Average: 11–25, 29–37, 41–46 Advanced: 11–20, 23–28, 30, 31, 33–46

REACHING ALL LEARNERS – Differentiated Instruction for students with

Developing Knowledge	On-level Knowledge	Advanced Knowledge	English Language Development
☐ Inclusion TE p. 471, 473	☐ Visual Cues TE p. 471	☐ Visual Cues TE p. 471	☐ Visual Cues TE p. 471
☐ Practice A 7-3 CRB	☐ Practice B 7-3 CRB	☐ Practice C 7-3 CRB	☐ Practice A, B, or C 7-3 CRB
☐ Reteach 7-3 CRB		☐ Challenge 7-3 CRB	☐ *Success for ELL* 7-3
☐ Homework Help Online Keyword: MR4 7-3	☐ Homework Help Online Keyword: MR4 7-3	☐ Homework Help Online Keyword: MR4 7-3	☐ Homework Help Online Keyword: MR4 7-3
☐ *Lesson Tutorial Video* 7-3	☐ *Lesson Tutorial Video* 7-3	☐ *Lesson Tutorial Video* 7-3	☐ *Lesson Tutorial Video* 7-3
☐ Reading Strategies 7-3 CRB	☐ Problem Solving 7-3 CRB	☐ Problem Solving 7-3 CRB	☐ Reading Strategies 7-3 CRB
☐ Questioning Strategies TE p. 471, 472	☐ Kinesthetic TE p. 473	☐ Algebra TE p. 475	
☐ *IDEA Works!* 7-3			☐ *Multilingual Glossary*

ASSESSMENT
☐ Lesson Quiz, TE p. 477 and Transparency 7-3
☐ State-Specific Test Prep Online Keyword: MR4 TestPrep

Holt Geometry

Teacher's Name _____ Class _____ Date _____

Lesson Plan 7-4
Applying Properties of Similar Triangles pp. 481–487   Day _____

Objectives Use properties of similar triangles to find segment lengths. Apply proportionality and triangle angle bisector theorems.

> **NCTM Standards:** students should apply appropriate techniques, tools, and formulas to determine measurements.

Pacing
☐ 45-minute Classes: 1 day   ☐ 90-minute Classes: 1/2 day ☐ Other_____

WARM UP
☐ Warm Up TE p. 481 and Warm Up Transparency 7-4
☐ Countdown to Testing Transparency, Week 16

TEACH
☐ Lesson Presentation CD-ROM 7-4
☐ Alternate Opener, Exploration Transparency 7-4, TE p. 481
☐ Reaching All Learners TE p. 482
☐ Additional Examples Transparencies 7-4
☐ Teaching Transparency 7-4
☐ *Know-It Notebook* 7-4

PRACTICE AND APPLY
☐ Examples 1-2: Basic: 8–11, 23 Average: 8–11, 23, 30 Advanced: 8–11, 23, 30
☐ Examples 1-4: Basic: 8–20, 22, 26, 28, 30, 32–35, 40–45 Average: 8–18, 21–23, 25–27, 29–36, 40–45 Advanced: 8–16, 21–45

REACHING ALL LEARNERS – Differentiated Instruction for students with

Developing Knowledge	On-level Knowledge	Advanced Knowledge	English Language Development
☐ Kinesthetic Experience TE p. 482	☐ Kinesthetic Experience TE p. 482	☐ Kinesthetic Experience TE p. 482	☐ Kinesthetic Experience TE p. 482
☐ Practice A 7-4 CRB	☐ Practice B 7-4 CRB	☐ Practice C 7-4 CRB	☐ Practice A, B, or C 7-4 CRB
☐ Reteach 7-4 CRB		☐ Challenge 7-4 CRB	☐ *Success for ELL* 7-4
☐ Homework Help Online Keyword: MR4 7-4	☐ Homework Help Online Keyword: MR4 7-4	☐ Homework Help Online Keyword: MR4 7-4	☐ Homework Help Online Keyword: MR4 7-4
☐ *Lesson Tutorial Video* 7-4	☐ *Lesson Tutorial Video* 7-4	☐ *Lesson Tutorial Video* 7-4	☐ *Lesson Tutorial Video* 7-4
☐ Reading Strategies 7-4 CRB	☐ Problem Solving 7-4 CRB	☐ Problem Solving 7-4 CRB	☐ Reading Strategies 7-4 CRB
☐ Questioning Strategies TE p. 482, 483	☐ Reading Math TE p. 483	☐ Critical Thinking TE p. 482, 485	
☐ *IDEA Works!* 7-4			☐ *Multilingual Glossary*

ASSESSMENT
☐ Lesson Quiz, TE p. 487 and Transparency 7-4
☐ State-Specific Test Prep Online Keyword: MR4 TestPrep

Holt Geometry

Lesson Plan 7-5

Using Proportional Relationships pp. 488–494   Day _____

Objectives Use ratios to make indirect measurements. Use scale drawings to solve problems.

> **NCTM Standards:** students should understand numbers, ways of representing numbers, relationships among numbers, and number systems.

Pacing
☐ 45-minute Classes: 1 day   ☐ 90-minute Classes: 1/2 day   ☐ Other_____

WARM UP
☐ Warm Up TE p. 488 and Warm Up Transparency 7-5
☐ Countdown to Testing Transparency, Week 16

TEACH
☐ Lesson Presentation CD-ROM 7-5
☐ Alternate Opener, Exploration Transparency 7-5, TE p. 488
☐ Reaching All Learners TE p. 489
☐ Additional Examples Transparencies 7-5
☐ Teaching Transparency 7-5
☐ *Know-It Notebook* 7-5

PRACTICE AND APPLY
☐ Examples 1-2: Basic: 12–15, 20–23, 27, 32 Average: 12–15, 20–23, 27, 32 Advanced: 12–15, 20–23, 27, 32, 33, 43
☐ Examples 1-4: Basic: 12–31, 36, 37, 39–42, 47–52 Average: 12–31, 35–43, 47–52 Advanced: 12–22, 26–52

REACHING ALL LEARNERS – Differentiated Instruction for students with

Developing Knowledge	On-level Knowledge	Advanced Knowledge	English Language Development
☐ Inclusion TE p. 491	☐ Cooperative Learning TE p. 489	☐ Cooperative Learning TE p. 489	☐ Cooperative Learning TE p. 489
☐ Practice A 7-5 CRB	☐ Practice B 7-5 CRB	☐ Practice C 7-5 CRB	☐ Practice A, B, or C 7-5 CRB
☐ Reteach 7-5 CRB		☐ Challenge 7-5 CRB	☐ *Success for ELL* 7-5
☐ Homework Help Online Keyword: MR4 7-5	☐ Homework Help Online Keyword: MR4 7-5	☐ Homework Help Online Keyword: MR4 7-5	☐ Homework Help Online Keyword: MR4 7-5
☐ *Lesson Tutorial Video* 7-5	☐ *Lesson Tutorial Video* 7-5	☐ *Lesson Tutorial Video* 7-5	☐ *Lesson Tutorial Video* 7-5
☐ Reading Strategies 7-5 CRB	☐ Problem Solving 7-5 CRB	☐ Problem Solving 7-5 CRB	☐ Reading Strategies 7-5 CRB
☐ Questioning Strategies TE p. 489, 490	☐ Auditory TE p. 490	☐ Critical Thinking TE p. 494	☐ Vocabulary Exercises SE p. 488
☐ *IDEA Works!* 7-5			☐ *Multilingual Glossary*

ASSESSMENT
☐ Lesson Quiz, TE p. 494 and Transparency 7-5
☐ State-Specific Test Prep Online Keyword: MR4 TestPrep

Holt Geometry

Lesson Plan 7-6
Dilations and Similarity in the Coordinate Plane pp. 495–500   Day _____

Objectives Apply similarity properties in the coordinate plane. Use coordinate proof to prove figures similar.

NCTM Standards: students should analyze change in various contexts.

Pacing
☐ 45-minute Classes: 1 day   ☐ 90-minute Classes: 1/2 day   ☐ Other_____

WARM UP
☐ Warm Up TE p. 495 and Warm Up Transparency 7-6
☐ Countdown to Testing Transparency, Week 16

TEACH
☐ Lesson Presentation CD-ROM 7-6
☐ Alternate Opener, Exploration Transparency 7-6, TE p. 495
☐ Reaching All Learners TE p. 496
☐ Additional Examples Transparencies 7-6
☐ *Geometry Lab Activities* 7-6
☐ *Know-It Notebook* 7-6

PRACTICE AND APPLY
☐ Examples 1-2: Basic: 10–12, 14 Average: 10–12, 14, 25 Advanced: 10–12, 14, 25, 26
☐ Examples 1-4: Basic: 10–16, 18, 20–24, 30–35 Average: 10–24, 29–35 Advanced: 10–35

REACHING ALL LEARNERS – Differentiated Instruction for students with

Developing Knowledge	On-level Knowledge	Advanced Knowledge	English Language Development
☐ Kinesthetic Experience TE p. 496	☐ Kinesthetic Experience TE p. 496	☐ Kinesthetic Experience TE p. 496	☐ Kinesthetic Experience TE p. 496
☐ Practice A 7-6 CRB	☐ Practice B 7-6 CRB	☐ Practice C 7-6 CRB	☐ Practice A, B, or C 7-6 CRB
☐ Reteach 7-6 CRB		☐ Challenge 7-6 CRB	☐ *Success for ELL* 7-6
☐ Homework Help Online Keyword: MR4 7-6	☐ Homework Help Online Keyword: MR4 7-6	☐ Homework Help Online Keyword: MR4 7-6	☐ Homework Help Online Keyword: MR4 7-6
☐ *Lesson Tutorial Video* 7-6	☐ *Lesson Tutorial Video* 7-6	☐ *Lesson Tutorial Video* 7-6	☐ *Lesson Tutorial Video* 7-6
☐ Reading Strategies 7-6 CRB	☐ Problem Solving 7-6 CRB	☐ Problem Solving 7-6 CRB	☐ Reading Strategies 7-6 CRB
☐ Questioning Strategies TE p. 496, 497	☐ Critical Thinking TE p. 496	☐ Multiple Representations TE p. 497	☐ Vocabulary Exercises SE p. 495
☐ *IDEA Works!* 7-6			☐ *Multilingual Glossary*

ASSESSMENT
☐ Lesson Quiz, TE p. 500 and Transparency 7-6
☐ State-Specific Test Prep Online Keyword: MR4 TestPrep

Holt Geometry

Teacher's Name _____ Class _____ Date _____

Lesson Plan 8-1
Similarity in Right Triangles pp. 518–523   Day _____

Objectives Use geometric mean to find segment lengths in right triangles. Apply similarity relationships in right triangles to solve problems.

> **NCTM Standards:** students should understand meanings of operations and how they relate to one another.

Pacing
☐ 45-minute Classes: 1 day   ☐ 90-minute Classes: 1/2 day   ☐ Other_____

WARM UP
☐ Warm Up TE p. 518 and Warm Up Transparency 8-1
☐ Countdown to Testing Transparency, Week 17

TEACH
☐ Lesson Presentation CD-ROM 8-1
☐ Alternate Opener, Exploration Transparency 8-1, TE p. 518
☐ Reaching All Learners TE p. 519
☐ Additional Examples Transparencies 8-1
☐ Teaching Transparency 8-1
☐ *Geometry Lab Activities* 8-1
☐ *Know-It Notebook* 8-1

PRACTICE AND APPLY
☐ Examples 1-2: Basic: 15–23, 28, 29 Average: 15–23, 28, 29, 45 Advanced: 15–23, 28, 29, 45, 46
☐ Examples 1-4: Basic: 15–37, 41, 44, 47–49, 54–62 Average: 15–27, 30–38 even, 39–50, 54–62
    Advanced: 15–27, 28–40 even, 42–62

REACHING ALL LEARNERS – Differentiated Instruction for students with

Developing Knowledge	On-level Knowledge	Advanced Knowledge	English Language Development
☐ Inclusion TE p. 521	☐ Concrete Manipulatives TE p. 519	☐ Concrete Manipulatives TE p. 519	☐ Concrete Manipulatives TE p. 519
☐ Practice A 8-1 CRB	☐ Practice B 8-1 CRB	☐ Practice C 8-1 CRB	☐ Practice A, B, or C 8-1 CRB
☐ Reteach 8-1 CRB		☐ Challenge 8-1 CRB	☐ *Success for ELL* 8-1
☐ Homework Help Online Keyword: MR4 8-1	☐ Homework Help Online Keyword: MR4 8-1	☐ Homework Help Online Keyword: MR4 8-1	☐ Homework Help Online Keyword: MR4 8-1
☐ *Lesson Tutorial Video* 8-1	☐ *Lesson Tutorial Video* 8-1	☐ *Lesson Tutorial Video* 8-1	☐ *Lesson Tutorial Video* 8-1
☐ Reading *Strategies* 8-1 CRB	☐ Problem Solving 8-1 CRB	☐ Problem Solving 8-1 CRB	☐ Reading *Strategies* 8-1 CRB
☐ Questioning Strategies TE p. 519, 520	☐ Visual TE p. 521	☐ Algebra TE p. 522	☐ Vocabulary Exercises SE p. 518
☐ *IDEA Works!* 8-1			☐ *Multilingual Glossary*

ASSESSMENT
☐ Lesson Quiz, TE p. 523 and Transparency 8-1
☐ State-Specific Test Prep Online Keyword: MR4 TestPrep

Holt Geometry

Lesson Plan 8-2

Trigonometric Ratios pp. 525–532   Day _____

Objectives Find the sine, cosine, and tangent of an acute angle. Use trigonometric ratios to find side lengths in right triangles and to solve real-world problems.

> **NCTM Standards:** students should understand numbers, ways of representing numbers, relationships among numbers, and number systems.

Pacing
☐ 45-minute Classes: 1 day   ☐ 90-minute Classes: 1/2 day   ☐ Other_____

WARM UP
☐ Warm Up TE p. 525 and Warm Up Transparency 8-2
☐ Countdown to Testing Transparency, Week 17

TEACH
☐ Lesson Presentation CD-ROM 8-2
☐ Alternate Opener, Exploration Transparency 8-2, TE p. 525
☐ Reaching All Learners TE p. 224
☐ Additional Examples Transparencies 8-2
☐ Teaching Transparency 8-2
☐ *Technology Lab Activities* 8-2
☐ *Know-It Notebook* 8-2

PRACTICE AND APPLY
☐ Examples 1-3: Basic: 22–36, 44–47, 56 Average: 22–36, 44–47, 56–61 Advanced: 22–36, 44–47, 56–61, 75–77
☐ Examples 1-5: Basic: 22–43, 48–50, 52, 53, 56, 58, 62–65, 68–70, 78–86 Average: 22–43, 44–50 even, 51, 52, 57–72, 78–86 Advanced: 22–43, 45, 47–86

REACHING ALL LEARNERS – Differentiated Instruction for students with

Developing Knowledge	On-level Knowledge	Advanced Knowledge	English Language Development
☐ Inclusion TE p. 526, 528	☐ Kinesthetic Experience TE p. 526	☐ Kinesthetic Experience TE p. 526	☐ Kinesthetic Experience TE p. 526
☐ Practice A 8-2 CRB	☐ Practice B 8-2 CRB	☐ Practice C 8-2 CRB	☐ Practice A, B, or C 8-2 CRB
☐ Reteach 8-2 CRB		☐ Challenge 8-2 CRB	☐ *Success for ELL* 8-2
☐ Homework Help Online Keyword: MR4 8-2	☐ Homework Help Online Keyword: MR4 8-2	☐ Homework Help Online Keyword: MR4 8-2	☐ Homework Help Online Keyword: MR4 8-2
☐ *Lesson Tutorial Video* 8-2	☐ *Lesson Tutorial Video* 8-2	☐ *Lesson Tutorial Video* 8-2	☐ *Lesson Tutorial Video* 8-2
☐ Reading Strategies 8-2 CRB	☐ Problem Solving 8-2 CRB	☐ Problem Solving 8-2 CRB	☐ Reading Strategies 8-2 CRB
☐ Questioning Strategies TE p. 526, 527, 528	☐ Algebra TE p. 531	☐ Critical Thinking TE p. 529	☐ Vocabulary Exercises SE p. 525
☐ *IDEA Works!* 8-2			☐ *Multilingual Glossary*

ASSESSMENT
☐ Lesson Quiz, TE p. 532 and Transparency 8-2
☐ State-Specific Test Prep Online Keyword: MR4 TestPrep

Holt Geometry

Lesson Plan 8-3
Solving Right Triangles pp. 534–541 Day _____

Objective Use trigonometric ratios to find angle measures in right triangles and to solve real-world problems.

> **NCTM Standards:** students should represent and analyze mathematical situations and structures using algebraic symbols.

Pacing
☐ 45-minute Classes: 1 day   ☐ 90-minute Classes: 1/2 day   ☐ Other_____

WARM UP
☐ Warm Up TE p. 534 and Warm Up Transparency 8-3
☐ Countdown to Testing Transparency, Week 18

TEACH
☐ Lesson Presentation CD-ROM 8-3
☐ Alternate Opener, Exploration Transparency 8-3, TE p. 534
☐ Reaching All Learners TE p. 535
☐ Additional Examples Transparencies 8-3
☐ Teaching Transparency 8-3
☐ *Know-It Notebook* 8-3

PRACTICE AND APPLY
☐ Examples 1-3: Basic: 21–35, 39–44, 48–50 Average: 21–35, 39–44, 48–50, 54, 56 Advanced: 21–35, 39–44, 48–50, 54, 56, 69, 76
☐ Examples 1-5: Basic: 21–39, 42, 47–57, 59, 62, 63, 65–68, 77–85 Average: 21–39, 42, 45–49, 53–63, 65–69, 74, 77–85 Advanced: 21–47, 51–54, 56, 58, 60, 61, 63–85

REACHING ALL LEARNERS – Differentiated Instruction for students with

Developing Knowledge	On-level Knowledge	Advanced Knowledge	English Language Development
☐ Inclusion TE p. 536, 538	☐ Auditory Cues TE p. 535	☐ Auditory Cues TE p. 535	☐ Auditory Cues TE p. 535
☐ Practice A 8-3 CRB	☐ Practice B 8-3 CRB	☐ Practice C 8-3 CRB	☐ Practice A, B, or C 8-3 CRB
☐ Reteach 8-3 CRB		☐ Challenge 8-3 CRB	☐ *Success for ELL* 8-3
☐ Homework Help Online Keyword: MR4 8-3	☐ Homework Help Online Keyword: MR4 8-3	☐ Homework Help Online Keyword: MR4 8-3	☐ Homework Help Online Keyword: MR4 8-3
☐ *Lesson Tutorial Video* 8-3	☐ *Lesson Tutorial Video* 8-3	☐ *Lesson Tutorial Video* 8-3	☐ *Lesson Tutorial Video* 8-3
☐ Reading Strategies 8-3 CRB	☐ Problem Solving 8-3 CRB	☐ Problem Solving 8-3 CRB	☐ Reading Strategies 8-3 CRB
☐ Questioning Strategies TE p. 535, 536	☐ Critical Thinking TE p. 540	☐ Technology TE p. 535	
☐ *IDEA Works!* 8-3			☐ *Multilingual Glossary*

ASSESSMENT
☐ Lesson Quiz, TE p. 541 and Transparency 8-3
☐ State-Specific Test Prep Online Keyword: MR4 TestPrep

Holt Geometry

Lesson Plan 8-4

Angles of Elevation and Depression pp. 544–549 Day _____

Objective Solve problems involving angles of elevation and angles of depression.

NCTM Standards: students should understand patterns, relations, and functions.

Pacing
☐ 45-minute Classes: 1 day   ☐ 90-minute Classes: 1/2 day   ☐ Other_____

WARM UP
☐ Warm Up TE p. 544 and Warm Up Transparency 8-4
☐ Countdown to Testing Transparency, Week 18

TEACH
☐ Lesson Presentation CD-ROM 8-4
☐ Alternate Opener, Exploration Transparency 8-4, TE p. 544
☐ Reaching All Learners TE p. 545
☐ Additional Examples Transparencies 8-4
☐ Teaching Transparency 8-4
☐ *Know-It Notebook* 8-4

PRACTICE AND APPLY
☐ Examples 1-2: Basic: 10–14, 17, 21, 22 Average: 10–14, 17–19, 21, 22 Advanced: 10–14, 17–19, 21, 22, 25
☐ Examples 1-4: Basic: 10–22, 24, 27–30, 35–43 Average: 10–31, 35–43 Advanced: 10–43

REACHING ALL LEARNERS – Differentiated Instruction for students with

Developing Knowledge	On-level Knowledge	Advanced Knowledge	English Language Development
☐ Modeling TE p. 545	☐ Modeling TE p. 545	☐ Modeling TE p. 545	☐ Modeling TE p. 545
☐ Practice A 8-4 CRB	☐ Practice B 8-4 CRB	☐ Practice C 8-4 CRB	☐ Practice A, B, or C 8-4 CRB
☐ Reteach 8-4 CRB		☐ Challenge 8-4 CRB	☐ *Success for ELL* 8-4
☐ Homework Help Online Keyword: MR4 8-4	☐ Homework Help Online Keyword: MR4 8-4	☐ Homework Help Online Keyword: MR4 8-4	☐ Homework Help Online Keyword: MR4 8-4
☐ *Lesson Tutorial Video* 8-4	☐ *Lesson Tutorial Video* 8-4	☐ *Lesson Tutorial Video* 8-4	☐ *Lesson Tutorial Video* 8-4
☐ Reading Strategies 8-4 CRB	☐ Problem Solving 8-4 CRB	☐ Problem Solving 8-4 CRB	☐ Reading Strategies 8-4 CRB
☐ Questioning Strategies TE p. 545, 546	☐ Communicating Math TE p. 548	☐ Science Link TE p. 547	☐ Vocabulary Exercises SE p. 544
☐ *IDEA Works!* 8-4			☐ *Multilingual Glossary*

ASSESSMENT
☐ Lesson Quiz, TE p. 549 and Transparency 8-4
☐ State-Specific Test Prep Online Keyword: MR4 TestPrep

Holt Geometry

Teacher's Name _____ Class _____ Date _____

Lesson Plan 8-5
Law of Sines and Law of Cosines pp. 551–558   *Day* _____

Objective Use the Law of Sines and the Law of Cosines to solve triangles.

> **NCTM Standards:** students should apply appropriate techniques, tools, and formulas to determine
> measurements.

Pacing
☐ 45-minute Classes: 1 day   ☐ 90-minute Classes: 1/2 day   ☐ Other_____

WARM UP
☐ Warm Up TE p. 551 and Warm Up Transparency 8-5
☐ Countdown to Testing Transparency, Week 18

TEACH
☐ Lesson Presentation CD-ROM 8-5
☐ Alternate Opener, Exploration Transparency 8-5, TE p. 551
☐ Reaching All Learners TE p. 552
☐ Additional Examples Transparencies 8-5
☐ Teaching Transparency 8-5
☐ *Know-It Notebook* 8-5

PRACTICE AND APPLY
☐ Examples 1-2: Basic: 14–31, 39, 42 Average: 14–31, 39, 42, 47 Advanced: 14–31, 39, 42, 47, 48
☐ Examples 1-4: Basic: 14–42, 46–48, 50–54, 56, 58–61, 65–74 Average: 14–51, 56, 58–61, 64–74
     Advanced: 14–50, 54, 55, 57–74

REACHING ALL LEARNERS – Differentiated Instruction for students with

Developing Knowledge	On-level Knowledge	Advanced Knowledge	English Language Development
☐ Inclusion TE p. 555	☐ Cognitive Strategies TE p. 552	☐ Cognitive Strategies TE p. 552	☐ Cognitive Strategies TE p. 552
☐ Practice A 8-5 CRB	☐ Practice B 8-5 CRB	☐ Practice C 8-5 CRB	☐ Practice A, B, or C 8-5 CRB
☐ Reteach 8-5 CRB		☐ Challenge 8-5 CRB	☐ *Success for ELL* 8-5
☐ Homework Help Online Keyword: MR4 8-5	☐ Homework Help Online Keyword: MR4 8-5	☐ Homework Help Online Keyword: MR4 8-5	☐ Homework Help Online Keyword: MR4 8-5
☐ *Lesson Tutorial Video* 8-5	☐ *Lesson Tutorial Video* 8-5	☐ *Lesson Tutorial Video* 8-5	☐ *Lesson Tutorial Video* 8-5
☐ Reading Strategies 8-5 CRB	☐ Problem Solving 8-5 CRB	☐ Problem Solving 8-5 CRB	☐ Reading Strategies 8-5 CRB
☐ Questioning Strategies TE p. 552, 553, 554	☐ Visual TE p. 556	☐ Technology TE p. 556	
☐ *IDEA Works!* 8-5			☐ *Multilingual Glossary*

ASSESSMENT
☐ Lesson Quiz, TE p. 558 and Transparency 8-5
☐ State-Specific Test Prep Online Keyword: MR4 TestPrep

Holt Geometry

Teacher's Name _____ Class _____ Date _____

Lesson Plan 8-6

Vectors pp. 559–567   Day _____

Objectives Find the magnitude and direction of a vector. Use vectors and vector addition to solve real-world problems.

> **NCTM Standards:** students should understand measurable attributes of objects and the units, systems, and processes of measurement.

Pacing
☐ 45-minute Classes: 1 day   ☐ 90-minute Classes: 1/2 day   ☐ Other_____

WARM UP
☐ Warm Up TE p. 559 and Warm Up Transparency 8-6
☐ Countdown to Testing Transparency, Week 18

TEACH
☐ Lesson Presentation CD-ROM 8-6
☐ Alternate Opener, Exploration Transparency 8-6, TE p. 559
☐ Reaching All Learners TE p. 560
☐ Additional Examples Transparencies 8-6
☐ *Know-It Notebook* 8-6

PRACTICE AND APPLY
☐ Examples 1-3: Basic: 18–26, 38–41, 45–48 Average: 18–26, 38–41, 44–48, 64 Advanced: 18–26, 38–41, 44–48, 64, 65
☐ Examples 1-5: Basic: 18–32, 34, 37–41, 44–48, 50, 53, 54, 59–63, 69–76 Average: 18–32, 34, 36–40, 43, 44, 50–56, 58–64, 69–76 Advanced: 18–39, 42–44, 46, 48–50, 54, 56–76

REACHING ALL LEARNERS – Differentiated Instruction for students with

Developing Knowledge	On-level Knowledge	Advanced Knowledge	English Language Development
☐ Inclusion TE p. 562	☐ Multiple Representations TE p. 560	☐ Multiple Representations TE p. 560	☐ Multiple Representations TE p. 560
☐ Practice A 8-6 CRB	☐ Practice B 8-6 CRB	☐ Practice C 8-6 CRB	☐ Practice A, B, or C 8-6 CRB
☐ Reteach 8-6 CRB		☐ Challenge 8-6 CRB	☐ *Success for ELL* 8-6
☐ Homework Help Online Keyword: MR4 8-6	☐ Homework Help Online Keyword: MR4 8-6	☐ Homework Help Online Keyword: MR4 8-6	☐ Homework Help Online Keyword: MR4 8-6
☐ *Lesson Tutorial Video* 8-6	☐ *Lesson Tutorial Video* 8-6	☐ *Lesson Tutorial Video* 8-6	☐ *Lesson Tutorial Video* 8-6
☐ Reading Strategies 8-6 CRB	☐ Problem Solving 8-6 CRB	☐ Problem Solving 8-6 CRB	☐ Reading Strategies 8-6 CRB
☐ Questioning Strategies TE p. 560, 561, 562	☐ Multiple Representations TE p. 563	☐ Probability TE p. 565	☐ Vocabulary Exercises SE p. 559
☐ *IDEA Works!* 8-6			☐ *Multilingual Glossary*

ASSESSMENT
☐ Lesson Quiz, TE p. 567 and Transparency 8-6
☐ State-Specific Test Prep Online Keyword: MR4 TestPrep

Holt Geometry

Teacher's Name _____ Class _____ Date _____

Lesson Plan 9-1
Developing Formulas for Triangles and Quadrilaterals pp. 589–597   Day _____

Objectives Develop and apply the formulas for the areas of triangles and special quadrilaterals. Solve problems involving perimeters and areas of triangles and special quadrilaterals.

NCTM Standards: students should analyze change in various contexts.

Pacing
☐ 45-minute Classes: 1 day   ☐ 90-minute Classes: 1/2 day   ☐ Other_____

WARM UP
☐ Warm Up TE p. 589 and Warm Up Transparency 9-1
☐ Countdown to Testing Transparency, Week 19

TEACH
☐ Lesson Presentation CD-ROM 9-1
☐ Alternate Opener, Exploration Transparency 9-1, TE p. 589
☐ Reaching All Learners TE p. 590
☐ Additional Examples Transparencies 9-1
☐ Teaching Transparency 9-1
☐ *Geometry Lab Activities* 9-1
☐ *Know-It Notebook* 9-1

PRACTICE AND APPLY
☐ Examples 1-2: Basic: 11–16, 20–26, 28–39 Average: 11–16, 20–26, 28–39, 41, 43–45 Advanced:
11–16, 20–26, 28–39, 41, 43–45, 55–57
☐ Examples 1-4: Basic: 11–40, 46, 47, 50–54, 60–67 Average: 11–32, 37–41, 43, 46–55, 60–67
Advanced: 11–27, 28–36 even, 41–45, 48–67

REACHING ALL LEARNERS – Differentiated Instruction for students with

Developing Knowledge	On-level Knowledge	Advanced Knowledge	English Language Development
☐ Inclusion TE p. 592, 596	☐ Concrete Manipulatives TE p. 590	☐ Concrete Manipulatives TE p. 590	☐ Concrete Manipulatives TE p. 590
☐ Practice A 9-1 CRB	☐ Practice B 9-1 CRB	☐ Practice C 9-1 CRB	☐ Practice A, B, or C 9-1 CRB
☐ Reteach 9-1 CRB		☐ Challenge 9-1 CRB	☐ *Success for ELL* 9-1
☐ Homework Help Online Keyword: MR4 9-1	☐ Homework Help Online Keyword: MR4 9-1	☐ Homework Help Online Keyword: MR4 9-1	☐ Homework Help Online Keyword: MR4 9-1
☐ *Lesson Tutorial Video* 9-1	☐ *Lesson Tutorial Video* 9-1	☐ *Lesson Tutorial Video* 9-1	☐ *Lesson Tutorial Video* 9-1
☐ Reading *Strategies* 9-1 CRB	☐ Problem Solving 9-1 CRB	☐ Problem Solving 9-1 CRB	☐ Reading *Strategies* 9-1 CRB
☐ Questioning Strategies TE p. 590, 591, 592	☐ Visual TE p. 594	☐ Algebra TE p. 594	
☐ *IDEA Works!* 9-1			☐ *Multilingual Glossary*

ASSESSMENT
☐ Lesson Quiz, TE p. 597 and Transparency 9-1
☐ State-Specific Test Prep Online Keyword: MR4 TestPrep

Holt Geometry

Lesson Plan 9-2
Developing Formulas for Circles and Regular Polygons pp. 600–605 Day _____

Objectives Develop and apply the formulas for the area and circumference of a circle. Develop and apply the formula for the area of a regular polygon.

> **NCTM Standards:** students should apply transformations and use symmetry to analyze mathematical situations.

Pacing
☐ 45-minute Classes: 1 day   ☐ 90-minute Classes: 1/2 day   ☐ Other_____

WARM UP
☐ Warm Up TE p. 600 and Warm Up Transparency 9-2
☐ Countdown to Testing Transparency, Week 20

TEACH
☐ Lesson Presentation CD-ROM 9-2
☐ Alternate Opener, Exploration Transparency 9-2, TE p. 600
☐ Reaching All Learners TE p. 601
☐ Additional Examples Transparencies 9-2
☐ Teaching Transparency 9-2
☐ *Technology Lab Activities* 9-2
☐ *Know-It Notebook* 9-2

PRACTICE AND APPLY
☐ Examples 1-3: Basic: 10–26, 29–40, 43–45, 49–54 Average: 10–17, 18–24 even, 26–46, 49–54
Advanced: 10–17, 18–24 even, 26–32, 34–54

REACHING ALL LEARNERS – Differentiated Instruction for students with

Developing Knowledge	On-level Knowledge	Advanced Knowledge	English Language Development
☐ Inclusion TE p. 601	☐ Concrete Manipulatives TE p. 601	☐ Concrete Manipulatives TE p. 601	☐ Concrete Manipulatives TE p. 601
☐ Practice A 9-2 CRB	☐ Practice B 9-2 CRB	☐ Practice C 9-2 CRB	☐ Practice A, B, or C 9-2 CRB
☐ Reteach 9-2 CRB		☐ Challenge 9-2 CRB	☐ *Success for ELL* 9-2
☐ Homework Help Online Keyword: MR4 9-2	☐ Homework Help Online Keyword: MR4 9-2	☐ Homework Help Online Keyword: MR4 9-2	☐ Homework Help Online Keyword: MR4 9-2
☐ *Lesson Tutorial Video* 9-2	☐ *Lesson Tutorial Video* 9-2	☐ *Lesson Tutorial Video* 9-2	☐ *Lesson Tutorial Video* 9-2
☐ Reading Strategies 9-2 CRB	☐ Problem Solving 9-2 CRB	☐ Problem Solving 9-2 CRB	☐ Reading Strategies 9-2 CRB
☐ Questioning Strategies TE p. 601, 602	☐ Critical Thinking TE p. 603	☐ Critical Thinking TE p. 603	☐ Vocabulary Exercises SE p. 600
☐ *IDEA Works!* 9-2			☐ *Multilingual Glossary*

ASSESSMENT
☐ Lesson Quiz, TE p. 605 and Transparency 9-2
☐ State-Specific Test Prep Online Keyword: MR4 TestPrep

Holt Geometry

Lesson Plan 9-3
Composite Figures pp. 606–612　　　　*Day* _____

Objective Use the Area Addition Postulate to find the areas of composite figures. Use composite figures to estimate the areas of irregular shapes.

NCTM Standards: students should formulate questions that can be addressed with data and collect, organize, and display relevant data to answer them.

Pacing
☐ 45-minute Classes: 1 day　　　☐ 90-minute Classes: 1/2 day　☐ Other_____

WARM UP
☐ Warm Up TE p. 606 and Warm Up Transparency 9-3
☐ Countdown to Testing Transparency, Week 20

TEACH
☐ Lesson Presentation CD-ROM 9-3
☐ Alternate Opener, Exploration Transparency 9-3, TE p. 606
☐ Reaching All Learners TE p. 607
☐ Additional Examples Transparencies 9-3
☐ *Know-It Notebook* 9-3

PRACTICE AND APPLY
☐ Examples 1-2: Basic: 9–12, 16–19 Average: 9–12, 16–20 Advanced: 9–12, 16–20, 33
☐ Examples 1-4: Basic: 9–21, 23–28, 31–33, 37–42 Average: 9–34, 37–42 Advanced: 9–42

REACHING ALL LEARNERS – Differentiated Instruction for students with

Developing Knowledge	On-level Knowledge	Advanced Knowledge	English Language Development
☐ Cooperative Learning TE p. 607	☐ Cooperative Learning TE p. 607	☐ Cooperative Learning TE p. 607	☐ Cooperative Learning TE p. 607
☐ Practice A 9-3 CRB	☐ Practice B 9-3 CRB	☐ Practice C 9-3 CRB	☐ Practice A, B, or C 9-3 CRB
☐ Reteach 9-3 CRB		☐ Challenge 9-3 CRB	☐ *Success for ELL* 9-3
☐ Homework Help Online Keyword: MR4 9-3	☐ Homework Help Online Keyword: MR4 9-3	☐ Homework Help Online Keyword: MR4 9-3	☐ Homework Help Online Keyword: MR4 9-3
☐ *Lesson Tutorial Video* 9-3	☐ *Lesson Tutorial Video* 9-3	☐ *Lesson Tutorial Video* 9-3	☐ *Lesson Tutorial Video* 9-3
☐ Reading Strategies 9-3 CRB	☐ Problem Solving 9-3 CRB	☐ Problem Solving 9-3 CRB	☐ Reading Strategies 9-3 CRB
☐ Questioning Strategies TE p. 607, 608	☐ Reading Math TE p. 607, 611	☐ Reading Math TE p. 607, 611	☐ Vocabulary Exercises SE p. 606
☐ *IDEA Works!* 9-3			☐ *Multilingual Glossary*

ASSESSMENT
☐ Lesson Quiz, TE p. 612 and Transparency 9-3
☐ State-Specific Test Prep Online Keyword: MR4 TestPrep

Holt Geometry

Teacher's Name _____ Class _____ Date _____

Lesson Plan 9-4

Perimeter and Area in the Coordinate Plane pp. 616–621   *Day _____*

Objective Find the perimeters and areas of figures in a coordinate plane.

> **NCTM Standards:** students should use visualization, spatial reasoning, and geometric modeling to solve problems.

Pacing
☐ 45-minute Classes: 1 day   ☐ 90-minute Classes: 1/2 day ☐ Other_____

WARM UP
☐ Warm Up TE p. 616 and Warm Up Transparency 9-4
☐ Countdown to Testing Transparency, Week 20

TEACH
☐ Lesson Presentation CD-ROM 9-4
☐ Alternate Opener, Exploration Transparency 9-4, TE p. 616
☐ Reaching All Learners TE p. 617
☐ Additional Examples Transparencies 9-4
☐ *Know-It Notebook* 9-4

PRACTICE AND APPLY
☐ Examples 1-2: Basic: 10–15, 19, 20 Average: 10–15, 19, 20, 27 Advanced: 10–15, 19, 20, 27–30
☐ Examples 1-4: Basic: 10–20, 23–26, 32–37 Average: 10–27, 32–37 Advanced: 10–37

REACHING ALL LEARNERS – Differentiated Instruction for students with

Developing Knowledge	On-level Knowledge	Advanced Knowledge	English Language Development
☐ Modeling TE p. 617	☐ Modeling TE p. 617	☐ Modeling TE p. 617	☐ Modeling TE p. 617
☐ Practice A 9-4 CRB	☐ Practice B 9-4 CRB	☐ Practice C 9-4 CRB	☐ Practice A, B, or C 9-4 CRB
☐ Reteach 9-4 CRB		☐ Challenge 9-4 CRB	☐ *Success for ELL* 9-4
☐ Homework Help Online Keyword: MR4 9-4	☐ Homework Help Online Keyword: MR4 9-4	☐ Homework Help Online Keyword: MR4 9-4	☐ Homework Help Online Keyword: MR4 9-4
☐ *Lesson Tutorial Video* 9-4	☐ *Lesson Tutorial Video* 9-4	☐ *Lesson Tutorial Video* 9-4	☐ *Lesson Tutorial Video* 9-4
☐ Reading Strategies 9-4 CRB	☐ Problem Solving 9-4 CRB	☐ Problem Solving 9-4 CRB	☐ Reading Strategies 9-4 CRB
☐ Questioning Strategies TE p. 617, 618	☐ Critical Thinking TE p. 618	☐ Algebra TE p. 620	
☐ *IDEA Works!* 9-4			☐ *Multilingual Glossary*

ASSESSMENT
☐ Lesson Quiz, TE p. 621 and Transparency 9-4
☐ State-Specific Test Prep Online Keyword: MR4 TestPrep

Holt Geometry

Lesson Plan 9-5
Effects of Changing Dimensions Proportionally pp. 622–627   Day _____

Objectives Describe the effect on perimeter and area when one or more dimensions of a figure are changed. Apply the relationship between perimeter and area in problem solving.

> **NCTM Standards:** students should understand measurable attributes of objects and the units, systems, and processes of measurement.

Pacing
☐ 45-minute Classes: 1 day   ☐ 90-minute Classes: 1/2 day   ☐ Other_____

WARM UP
☐ Warm Up TE p. 622 and Warm Up Transparency 9-5
☐ Countdown to Testing Transparency, Week 21

TEACH
☐ Lesson Presentation CD-ROM 9-5
☐ Alternate Opener, Exploration Transparency 9-5, TE p. 622
☐ Reaching All Learners TE p. 623
☐ Additional Examples Transparencies 9-5
☐ Teaching Transparency 9-5
☐ *Technology Lab Activities* 9-5
☐ *Know-It Notebook* 9-5

PRACTICE AND APPLY
☐ Examples 1-2: Basic: 8–11, 15–22, 25, 26 Average: 8–11, 15–22, 25–27 Advanced: 8–11, 15–22, 25–27, 34–36
☐ Examples 1-4: Basic: 8–23, 25–27, 29–33, 37–43 Average: 8–21, 24–34, 37–43 Advanced: 8–15, 16–20 even, 21–43

REACHING ALL LEARNERS – Differentiated Instruction for students with

Developing Knowledge	On-level Knowledge	Advanced Knowledge	English Language Development
☐ Inclusion TE p. 625	☐ Communication TE p. 623	☐ Communication TE p. 623	☐ Communication TE p. 623
☐ Practice A 9-5 CRB	☐ Practice B 9-5 CRB	☐ Practice C 9-5 CRB	☐ Practice A, B, or C 9-5 CRB
☐ Reteach 9-5 CRB		☐ Challenge 9-5 CRB	☐ *Success for ELL* 9-5
☐ Homework Help Online Keyword: MR4 9-5	☐ Homework Help Online Keyword: MR4 9-5	☐ Homework Help Online Keyword: MR4 9-5	☐ Homework Help Online Keyword: MR4 9-5
☐ *Lesson Tutorial Video* 9-5	☐ *Lesson Tutorial Video* 9-5	☐ *Lesson Tutorial Video* 9-5	☐ *Lesson Tutorial Video* 9-5
☐ Reading Strategies 9-5 CRB	☐ Problem Solving 9-5 CRB	☐ Problem Solving 9-5 CRB	☐ Reading Strategies 9-5 CRB
☐ Questioning Strategies TE p. 623, 624	☐ Critical Thinking TE p. 623, 626	☐ Critical Thinking TE p. 623, 626	
☐ *IDEA Works!* 9-5			☐ *Multilingual Glossary*

ASSESSMENT
☐ Lesson Quiz, TE p. 627 and Transparency 9-5
☐ State-Specific Test Prep Online Keyword: MR4 TestPrep

Holt Geometry

Lesson Plan 9-6
Geometric Probability pp. 630–636   Day _____

Objectives Calculate geometric probabilities. Use geometric probability to predict results in real-world situations.

NCTM Standards: students should understand and apply basic concepts of probability.

Pacing
☐ 45-minute Classes: 1 day   ☐ 90-minute Classes: 1/2 day   ☐ Other_____

WARM UP
☐ Warm Up TE p. 630 and Warm Up Transparency 9-6
☐ Countdown to Testing Transparency, Week 21

TEACH
☐ Lesson Presentation CD-ROM 9-6
☐ Alternate Opener, Exploration Transparency 9-6, TE p. 630
☐ Reaching All Learners TE p. 631
☐ Additional Examples Transparencies 9-6
☐ Teaching Transparency 9-6
☐ *Know-It Notebook* 9-6

PRACTICE AND APPLY
☐ Examples 1-2: Basic: 16–22 Average: 16–22, 49 Advanced: 16–22, 49
☐ Examples 1-4: Basic: 16–31, 33–37, 44–47, 52–57 Average: 16–48, 52–57 Advanced: 16–31, 33–57

REACHING ALL LEARNERS – Differentiated Instruction for students with

Developing Knowledge	On-level Knowledge	Advanced Knowledge	English Language Development
☐ Kinesthetic Experience TE p. 631	☐ Kinesthetic Experience TE p. 631	☐ Kinesthetic Experience TE p. 631	☐ Kinesthetic Experience TE p. 631
☐ Practice A 9-6 CRB	☐ Practice B 9-6 CRB	☐ Practice C 9-6 CRB	☐ Practice A, B, or C 9-6 CRB
☐ Reteach 9-6 CRB		☐ Challenge 9-6 CRB	☐ *Success for ELL* 9-6
☐ Homework Help Online Keyword: MR4 9-6	☐ Homework Help Online Keyword: MR4 9-6	☐ Homework Help Online Keyword: MR4 9-6	☐ Homework Help Online Keyword: MR4 9-6
☐ *Lesson Tutorial Video* 9-6	☐ *Lesson Tutorial Video* 9-6	☐ *Lesson Tutorial Video* 9-6	☐ *Lesson Tutorial Video* 9-6
☐ Reading Strategies 9-6 CRB	☐ Problem Solving 9-6 CRB	☐ Problem Solving 9-6 CRB	☐ Reading Strategies 9-6 CRB
☐ Questioning Strategies TE p. 631, 632	☐ Kinesthetic TE p. 634	☐ Kinesthetic TE p. 634	☐ Vocabulary Exercises SE p. 630
☐ *IDEA Works!* 9-6			☐ *Multilingual Glossary*

ASSESSMENT
☐ Lesson Quiz, TE p. 636 and Transparency 9-6
☐ State-Specific Test Prep Online Keyword: MR4 TestPrep

Holt Geometry

Lesson Plan 10-1
Solid Geometry pp. 654–660   Day _____

Objectives Classify three-dimensional figures according to their properties. Use nets and cross sections to analyze three-dimensional figures.

NCTM Standards: students should understand patterns, relations, and functions.

Pacing
☐ 45-minute Classes: 1 day   ☐ 90-minute Classes: 1/2 day   ☐ Other_____

WARM UP
☐ Warm Up TE p. 654 and Warm Up Transparency 10-1
☐ Countdown to Testing Transparency, Week 22

TEACH
☐ Lesson Presentation CD-ROM 10-1
☐ Alternate Opener, Exploration Transparency 10-1, TE p. 654
☐ Reaching All Learners TE p. 655
☐ Additional Examples Transparencies 10-1
☐ Teaching Transparency 10-1
☐ *Know-It Notebook* 10-1

PRACTICE AND APPLY
☐ Examples 1-2: Basic: 13–18, 28–31 Average: 13–18, 28–32 Advanced: 13–18, 28–33
☐ Examples 1-4: Basic: 13–38, 41–44, 52–59 Average: 13–25, 26–32 even, 33–46, 52–59 Advanced: 13–23, 24–32 even, 33–37, 39–59

REACHING ALL LEARNERS – Differentiated Instruction for students with

Developing Knowledge	On-level Knowledge	Advanced Knowledge	English Language Development
☐ Concrete Manipulatives TE p. 655	☐ Concrete Manipulatives TE p. 655	☐ Concrete Manipulatives TE p. 655	☐ Concrete Manipulatives TE p. 655
☐ Practice A 10-1 CRB	☐ Practice B 10-1 CRB	☐ Practice C 10-1 CRB	☐ Practice A, B, or C 10-1 CRB
☐ Reteach 10-1 CRB		☐ Challenge 10-1 CRB	☐ *Success for ELL* 10-1
☐ Homework Help Online Keyword: MR4 10-1	☐ Homework Help Online Keyword: MR4 10-1	☐ Homework Help Online Keyword: MR4 10-1	☐ Homework Help Online Keyword: MR4 10-1
☐ *Lesson Tutorial Video* 10-1	☐ *Lesson Tutorial Video* 10-1	☐ *Lesson Tutorial Video* 10-1	☐ *Lesson Tutorial Video* 10-1
☐ Reading *Strategies* 10-1 CRB	☐ Problem Solving 10-1 CRB	☐ Problem Solving 10-1 CRB	☐ Reading *Strategies* 10-1 CRB
☐ Questioning Strategies TE p. 655, 656	☐ Kinesthetic TE p. 655, 657	☐ Auditory TE p. 655	☐ Vocabulary Exercises SE p. 654
☐ *IDEA Works!* 10-1			☐ *Multilingual Glossary*

ASSESSMENT
☐ Lesson Quiz, TE p. 660 and Transparency 10-1
☐ State-Specific Test Prep Online Keyword: MR4 TestPrep

Holt Geometry

Teacher's Name _____ Class _____ Date _____

Lesson Plan 10-2
Representations of Three-Dimensional Figures pp. 661–668   Day _____

Objectives Draw representations of three-dimensional figures. Recognize a three-dimensional figure from a given representation.

> **NCTM Standards:** students should analyze characteristics and properties of two-and three-dimensional geometric shapes and develop mathematical arguments about geometric relationships.

Pacing
☐ 45-minute Classes: 1 day   ☐ 90-minute Classes: 1/2 day   ☐ Other_____

WARM UP
☐ Warm Up TE p. 661 and Warm Up Transparency 10-2
☐ Countdown to Testing Transparency, Week 22

TEACH
☐ Lesson Presentation CD-ROM 10-2
☐ Alternate Opener, Exploration Transparency 10-2, TE p. 661
☐ Reaching All Learners TE p. 662
☐ Additional Examples Transparencies 10-2
☐ Teaching Transparency 10-2
☐ *Know-It Notebook* 10-2

PRACTICE AND APPLY
☐ Examples 1-2: Basic: 14–19, 27, 28, 30, 31 Average: 14–19, 27, 28, 30–32 Advanced: 14–19, 27, 28, 30–32, 41
☐ Examples 1-4: Basic: 14–32, 35–37, 43–51 Average: 14–39, 43–51 Advanced: 14–51

REACHING ALL LEARNERS – Differentiated Instruction for students with

Developing Knowledge	On-level Knowledge	Advanced Knowledge	English Language Development
☐ Inclusion TE p. 665	☐ Kinesthetic Experience TE p. 662	☐ Kinesthetic Experience TE p. 662	☐ Kinesthetic Experience TE p. 662
☐ Practice A 10-2 CRB	☐ Practice B 10-2 CRB	☐ Practice C 10-2 CRB	☐ Practice A, B, or C 10-2 CRB
☐ Reteach 10-2 CRB		☐ Challenge 10-2 CRB	☐ *Success for ELL* 10-2
☐ Homework Help Online Keyword: MR4 10-2	☐ Homework Help Online Keyword: MR4 10-2	☐ Homework Help Online Keyword: MR4 10-2	☐ Homework Help Online Keyword: MR4 10-2
☐ *Lesson Tutorial Video* 10-2	☐ *Lesson Tutorial Video* 10-2	☐ *Lesson Tutorial Video* 10-2	☐ *Lesson Tutorial Video* 10-2
☐ Reading Strategies 10-2 CRB	☐ Reading Strategies 10-2 CRB	☐ Reading Strategies 10-2 CRB	☐ Reading Strategies 10-2 CRB
☐ Questioning Strategies TE p. 662, 663, 664	☐ Visual TE p. 666	☐ Multiple Representations TE p. 662	☐ Vocabulary Exercises SE p. 661
☐ *IDEA Works!* 10-2			☐ *Multilingual Glossary*

ASSESSMENT
☐ Lesson Quiz, TE p. 668 and Transparency 10-2
☐ State-Specific Test Prep Online Keyword: MR4 TestPrep

Holt Geometry

Teacher's Name _____ Class _____ Date _____

Lesson Plan 10-3
Formulas in Three Dimensions pp. 670–677   *Day* _____

Objectives Apply Euler's formula to find the number of vertices, edges, and faces of a polyhedron. Develop and apply the Distance and Midpoint Formulas in three dimensions.

NCTM Standards: students should select and use appropriate statistical methods to analyze data.

Pacing
☐ 45-minute Classes: 1 day   ☐ 90-minute Classes: 1/2 day   ☐ Other_____

WARM UP
☐ Warm Up TE p. 670 and Warm Up Transparency 10-3
☐ Countdown to Testing Transparency, Week 22

TEACH
☐ Lesson Presentation CD-ROM 10-3
☐ Alternate Opener, Exploration Transparency 10-3, TE p. 670
☐ Reaching All Learners TE p. 671, 672
☐ Additional Examples Transparencies 10-3
☐ Teaching Transparency 10-3
☐ *Know-It Notebook* 10-3

PRACTICE AND APPLY
☐ Examples 1-3: Basic: 15–23, 28–33, 35–44, 52 Average: 15–23, 28–33, 35–44, 52, 53 Advanced: 15–23, 28–33, 35–44, 52, 53, 60
☐ Examples 1-5: Basic: 15–54, 57–69, 64–71 Average: 15–44, 46–50 even, 51–61, 64–71 Advanced: 15–44, 46–50 even, 51–71

REACHING ALL LEARNERS – Differentiated Instruction for students with

Developing Knowledge	On-level Knowledge	Advanced Knowledge	English Language Development
☐ Modeling TE p. 671	☐ Critical Thinking TE p. 672	☐ Critical Thinking TE p. 672	☐ Modeling TE p. 671
☐ Practice A 10-3 CRB	☐ Practice B 10-3 CRB	☐ Practice C 10-3 CRB	☐ Practice A, B, or C 10-3 CRB
☐ Reteach 10-3 CRB		☐ Challenge 10-3 CRB	☐ *Success for ELL* 10-3
☐ Homework Help Online Keyword: MR4 10-3	☐ Homework Help Online Keyword: MR4 10-3	☐ Homework Help Online Keyword: MR4 10-3	☐ Homework Help Online Keyword: MR4 10-3
☐ *Lesson Tutorial Video* 10-3	☐ *Lesson Tutorial Video* 10-3	☐ *Lesson Tutorial Video* 10-3	☐ *Lesson Tutorial Video* 10-3
☐ Reading Strategies 10-3 CRB	☐ Problem Solving 10-3 CRB	☐ Problem Solving 10-3 CRB	☐ Reading Strategies 10-3 CRB
☐ Questioning Strategies TE p. 671, 672, 673	☐ Visual TE p. 673	☐ Algebra TE p. 676	☐ Vocabulary Exercises SE p. 670
☐ *IDEA Works!* 10-3			☐ *Multilingual Glossary*

ASSESSMENT
☐ Lesson Quiz, TE p. 677 and Transparency 10-3
☐ State-Specific Test Prep Online Keyword: MR4 TestPrep

Holt Geometry

Teacher's Name _____ Class _____ Date _____

Lesson Plan 10-4
Surface Area of Prisms and Cylinders pp. 680–687   *Day* _____

Objectives Learn and apply the formula for the surface area of a prism. Learn and apply the formula for
the surface area of a cylinder.

NCTM Standards: students should understand measurable attributes of objects and the units, systems, and processes of measurement.

Pacing
☐ 45-minute Classes: 1 day   ☐ 90-minute Classes: 1/2 day   ☐ Other_____

WARM UP
☐ Warm Up TE p. 680 and Warm Up Transparency 10-4
☐ Countdown to Testing Transparency, Week 23

TEACH
☐ Lesson Presentation CD-ROM 10-4
☐ Alternate Opener, Exploration Transparency 10-4, TE p. 680
☐ Reaching All Learners TE p. 681
☐ Additional Examples Transparencies 10-4
☐ Teaching Transparency 10-4
☐ *Technology Lab Activities* 10-4
☐ *Know-It Notebook* 10-4

PRACTICE AND APPLY
☐ Examples 1-2: Basic: 13–18, 23–31 Average: 13–18, 23–31, 41 Advanced: 13–18, 23–31, 41, 43
☐ Examples 1-5: Basic: 13–34, 37–40, 44–50 Average: 13–41, 44–50 Advanced: 13–50

REACHING ALL LEARNERS – Differentiated Instruction for students with

Developing Knowledge	On-level Knowledge	Advanced Knowledge	English Language Development
☐ Inclusion TE p. 681	☐ Multiple Representations TE p. 681	☐ Multiple Representations TE p. 681	☐ Multiple Representations TE p. 681
☐ Practice A 10-4 CRB	☐ Practice B 10-4 CRB	☐ Practice C 10-4 CRB	☐ Practice A, B, or C 10-4 CRB
☐ Reteach 10-4 CRB		☐ Challenge 10-4 CRB	☐ *Success for ELL* 10-4
☐ Homework Help Online Keyword: MR4 10-4	☐ Homework Help Online Keyword: MR4 10-4	☐ Homework Help Online Keyword: MR4 10-4	☐ Homework Help Online Keyword: MR4 10-4
☐ *Lesson Tutorial Video* 10-4	☐ *Lesson Tutorial Video* 10-4	☐ *Lesson Tutorial Video* 10-4	☐ *Lesson Tutorial Video* 10-4
☐ Reading Strategies 10-4 CRB	☐ Problem Solving 10-4 CRB	☐ Problem Solving 10-4 CRB	☐ Reading Strategies 10-4 CRB
☐ Questioning Strategies TE p. 681, 682, 683	☐ Reading Math TE p. 681	☐ Communicating Math TE p. 682	☐ Vocabulary Exercises SE p. 680
☐ *IDEA Works!* 10-4			☐ *Multilingual Glossary*

ASSESSMENT
☐ Lesson Quiz, TE p. 687 and Transparency 10-4
☐ State-Specific Test Prep Online Keyword: MR4 TestPrep

Holt Geometry

Teacher's Name _____ Class _____ Date _____

Lesson Plan 10-5
Surface Area of Pyramids and Cones pp. 689–696   *Day* _____

Objectives Learn and apply the formula for the surface area of a cone. Learn and apply the formula for the surface area of a cone.

> **NCTM Standards:** students should apply transformations and use symmetry to analyze mathematical situations.

Pacing
☐ 45-minute Classes: 1 day   ☐ 90-minute Classes: 1/2 day   ☐ Other_____

WARM UP
☐ Warm Up TE p. 689 and Warm Up Transparency 10-5
☐ Countdown to Testing Transparency, Week 23

TEACH
☐ Lesson Presentation CD-ROM 10-5
☐ Alternate Opener, Exploration Transparency 10-5, TE p. 689
☐ Reaching All Learners TE p. 690, 691
☐ Additional Examples Transparencies 10-5
☐ Teaching Transparency 10-5
☐ *Geometry Lab Activities* 10-5
☐ *Know-It Notebook* 10-5

PRACTICE AND APPLY
☐ Examples 1-3: Basic: 13–20, 24–27 Average: 13–20, 24–27, 41 Advanced: 13–20, 24–27, 41, 42
☐ Examples 1-5: Basic: 13–35, 38–40, 44–52 Average: 13–41, 44–52 Advanced: 13–52

REACHING ALL LEARNERS – Differentiated Instruction for students with

Developing Knowledge	On-level Knowledge	Advanced Knowledge	English Language Development
☐ Cognitive Strategies TE p. 690, Kinesthetic Experience TE p. 691	☐ Cognitive Strategies TE p. 690, Kinesthetic Experience TE p. 691	☐ Cognitive Strategies TE p. 690, Kinesthetic Experience TE p. 691	☐ Cognitive Strategies TE p. 690, Kinesthetic Experience TE p. 691
☐ Practice A 10-5 CRB	☐ Practice B 10-5 CRB	☐ Practice C 10-5 CRB	☐ Practice A, B, or C 10-5 CRB
☐ Reteach 10-5 CRB		☐ Challenge 10-5 CRB	☐ *Success for ELL* 10-5
☐ Homework Help Online Keyword: MR4 10-5	☐ Homework Help Online Keyword: MR4 10-5	☐ Homework Help Online Keyword: MR4 10-5	☐ Homework Help Online Keyword: MR4 10-5
☐ *Lesson Tutorial Video* 10-5	☐ *Lesson Tutorial Video* 10-5	☐ *Lesson Tutorial Video* 10-5	☐ *Lesson Tutorial Video* 10-5
☐ Reading Strategies 10-5 CRB	☐ Problem Solving 10-5 CRB	☐ Problem Solving 10-5 CRB	☐ Reading Strategies 10-5 CRB
☐ Questioning Strategies TE p. 690, 691, 692	☐ Kinesthetic TE p. 694	☐ Kinesthetic TE p. 694	☐ Vocabulary Exercises SE p. 689
☐ *IDEA Works!* 10-5			☐ *Multilingual Glossary*

ASSESSMENT
☐ Lesson Quiz, TE p. 696 and Transparency 10-5
☐ State-Specific Test Prep Online Keyword: MR4 TestPrep

Holt Geometry

Teacher's Name _____ Class _____ Date _____

Lesson Plan 10-6
Volume of Prisms and Cylinders pp. 697–704   *Day* _____

Objectives Learn and apply the formula for the volume of a prism. Learn and apply the formula for the
volume of a cylinder.

NCTM Standards: students should apply transformations and use symmetry to analyze mathematical situations.

Pacing
☐ 45-minute Classes: 1 day   ☐ 90-minute Classes: 1/2 day   ☐ Other_____

WARM UP
☐ Warm Up TE p. 697 and Warm Up Transparency 10-6
☐ Countdown to Testing Transparency, Week 23

TEACH
☐ Lesson Presentation CD-ROM 10-6
☐ Alternate Opener, Exploration Transparency 10-6, TE p. 697
☐ Reaching All Learners TE p. 698
☐ Additional Examples Transparencies 10-6
☐ Teaching Transparency 10-6
☐ *Know-It Notebook* 10-6

PRACTICE AND APPLY
☐ Examples 1-3: Basic: 13–19, 24, 25, 27–34 Average: 13–19, 41 Advanced: 13–19, 41–43
☐ Examples 1-5: Basic: 13–34, 37–40, 45–52 Average: 13–41, 45–52 Advanced: 13–52

REACHING ALL LEARNERS – Differentiated Instruction for students with

Developing Knowledge	On-level Knowledge	Advanced Knowledge	English Language Development
☐ Cooperative Learning TE p. 698	☐ Cooperative Learning TE p. 698	☐ Cooperative Learning TE p. 698	☐ Cooperative Learning TE p. 698
☐ Practice A 10-6 CRB	☐ Practice B 10-6 CRB	☐ Practice C 10-6 CRB	☐ Practice A, B, or C 10-6 CRB
☐ Reteach 10-6 CRB		☐ Challenge 10-6 CRB	☐ *Success for ELL* 10-6
☐ Homework Help Online Keyword: MR4 10-6	☐ Homework Help Online Keyword: MR4 10-6	☐ Homework Help Online Keyword: MR4 10-6	☐ Homework Help Online Keyword: MR4 10-6
☐ *Lesson Tutorial Video* 10-6	☐ *Lesson Tutorial Video* 10-6	☐ *Lesson Tutorial Video* 10-6	☐ *Lesson Tutorial Video* 10-6
☐ Reading Strategies 10-6 CRB	☐ Problem Solving 10-6 CRB	☐ Problem Solving 10-6 CRB	☐ Reading Strategies 10-6 CRB
☐ Questioning Strategies TE p. 698, 699, 700	☐ Algebra TE p. 703	☐ Science Link TE p. 701	☐ Vocabulary Exercises SE p. 697
☐ *IDEA Works!* 10-6			☐ *Multilingual Glossary*

ASSESSMENT
☐ Lesson Quiz, TE p. 704 and Transparency 10-6
☐ State-Specific Test Prep Online Keyword: MR4 TestPrep

Holt Geometry

Lesson Plan 10-7
Volume of Pyramids and Cones pp. 705–712   Day _____

Objectives Learn and apply the formula for the volume of a pyramid. Learn and apply the formula for the volume of a cone.

> **NCTM Standards:** students should apply transformations and use symmetry to analyze mathematical situations.

Pacing
☐ 45-minute Classes: 1 day   ☐ 90-minute Classes: 1/2 day   ☐ Other_____

WARM UP
☐ Warm Up TE p. 705 and Warm Up Transparency 10-7
☐ Countdown to Testing Transparency, Week 23

TEACH
☐ Lesson Presentation CD-ROM 10-7
☐ Alternate Opener, Exploration Transparency 10-7, TE p. 705
☐ Reaching All Learners TE p. 706
☐ Additional Examples Transparencies 10-7
☐ Teaching Transparency 10-7
☐ *Know-It Notebook* 10-7

PRACTICE AND APPLY
☐ Examples 1-3: Basic: 13–19, 24–37 Average: 13–19, 24–37, 46 Advanced: 13–19, 24–37, 46–50
☐ Examples 1-5: Basic: 13–38, 41–45, 51–59 Average: 13–46, 51–59 Advanced: 13–37, 39–59

REACHING ALL LEARNERS – Differentiated Instruction for students with

Developing Knowledge	On-level Knowledge	Advanced Knowledge	English Language Development
☐ Concrete Manipulatives TE p. 706	☐ Concrete Manipulatives TE p. 706	☐ Concrete Manipulatives TE p. 706	☐ Concrete Manipulatives TE p. 706
☐ Practice A 10-7 CRB	☐ Practice B 10-7 CRB	☐ Practice C 10-7 CRB	☐ Practice A, B, or C 10-7 CRB
☐ Reteach 10-7 CRB		☐ Challenge 10-7 CRB	☐ *Success for ELL* 10-7
☐ Homework Help Online Keyword: MR4 10-7	☐ Homework Help Online Keyword: MR4 10-7	☐ Homework Help Online Keyword: MR4 10-7	☐ Homework Help Online Keyword: MR4 10-7
☐ *Lesson Tutorial Video* 10-7	☐ *Lesson Tutorial Video* 10-7	☐ *Lesson Tutorial Video* 10-7	☐ *Lesson Tutorial Video* 10-7
☐ Reading Strategies 10-7 CRB	☐ Problem Solving 10-7 CRB	☐ Problem Solving 10-7 CRB	☐ Reading Strategies 10-7 CRB
☐ Questioning Strategies TE p. 706, 707, 708	☐ Reading Math TE p. 710	☐ Reading Math TE p. 710	☐ Vocabulary Exercises SE p. 705
☐ *IDEA Works!* 10-7			☐ *Multilingual Glossary*

ASSESSMENT
☐ Lesson Quiz, TE p. 712 and Transparency 10-7
☐ State-Specific Test Prep Online Keyword: MR4 TestPrep

Holt Geometry

Lesson Plan 10-8
Spheres pp. 714–721   Day _____

Objective Learn and apply the formula for the volume of a sphere. Learn and apply the formula for the surface area of a sphere.

> **NCTM Standards:** students should apply appropriate techniques, tools, and formulas to determine measurements.

Pacing
☐ 45-minute Classes: 1 day   ☐ 90-minute Classes: 1/2 day   ☐ Other_____

WARM UP
☐ Warm Up TE p. 714 and Warm Up Transparency 10-8
☐ Countdown to Testing Transparency, Week 24

TEACH
☐ Lesson Presentation CD-ROM 10-8
☐ Alternate Opener, Exploration Transparency 10-8, TE p. 714
☐ Reaching All Learners TE p. 715
☐ Additional Examples Transparencies 10-8
☐ Teaching Transparency 10-8
☐ *Know-It Notebook* 10-8

PRACTICE AND APPLY
☐ Examples 1-3: Basic: 13–19, 24–27, 29–32, 34, 35–38 Average: 13–19, 24–27, 29–32, 34, 35–38, 45
    Advanced: 13–19, 24–27, 29–32, 34, 35–38, 45–48
☐ Examples 1-5: Basic: 13–38, 41–44, 49–54 Average: 13–45, 49–54 Advanced: 13–54

REACHING ALL LEARNERS – Differentiated Instruction for students with

Developing Knowledge	On-level Knowledge	Advanced Knowledge	English Language Development
☐ Curriculum Integration TE p. 715	☐ Curriculum Integration TE p. 715	☐ Curriculum Integration TE p. 715	☐ Curriculum Integration TE p. 715
☐ Practice A 10-8 CRB	☐ Practice B 10-8 CRB	☐ Practice C 10-8 CRB	☐ Practice A, B, or C 10-8 CRB
☐ Reteach 10-8 CRB		☐ Challenge 10-8 CRB	☐ *Success for ELL* 10-8
☐ Homework Help Online Keyword: MR4 10-8	☐ Homework Help Online Keyword: MR4 10-8	☐ Homework Help Online Keyword: MR4 10-8	☐ Homework Help Online Keyword: MR4 10-8
☐ *Lesson Tutorial Video* 10-8	☐ *Lesson Tutorial Video* 10-8	☐ *Lesson Tutorial Video* 10-8	☐ *Lesson Tutorial Video* 10-8
☐ Reading Strategies 10-8 CRB	☐ Problem Solving 10-8 CRB	☐ Problem Solving 10-8 CRB	☐ Reading Strategies 10-8 CRB
☐ Questioning Strategies TE p. 715, 716, 717	☐ Social Studies Link TE p. 720	☐ Social Studies Link TE p. 720	☐ Vocabulary Exercises SE p. 714
☐ *IDEA Works!* 10-8			☐ *Multilingual Glossary*

ASSESSMENT
☐ Lesson Quiz, TE p. 721 and Transparency 10-8
☐ State-Specific Test Prep Online Keyword: MR4 TestPrep

Holt Geometry

Teacher's Name _____ Class _____ Date _____

Lesson Plan 11-1
Lines That Intersect Circles pp. 746–754   Day _____

Objectives Identify tangents, secants, and chords. Use properties of tangents to solve problems.

NCTM Standards: students should analyze characteristics and properties of two-and three-dimensional geometric shapes and develop mathematical arguments about geometric relationships.

Pacing
☐ 45-minute Classes: 1 day   ☐ 90-minute Classes: 1/2 day   ☐ Other_____

WARM UP
☐ Warm Up TE p. 746 and Warm Up Transparency 11-1

TEACH
☐ Lesson Presentation CD-ROM 11-1
☐ Alternate Opener, Exploration Transparency 11-1, TE p. 746
☐ Reaching All Learners TE p. 747
☐ Additional Examples Transparencies 11-1
☐ Teaching Transparency 11-1
☐ *Know-It Notebook* 11-1

PRACTICE AND APPLY
☐ Examples 1-2: Basic: 11–14, 18, 19, 22–24 Average: 11–14, 18, 19, 22–25 Advanced: 11–14, 18, 19, 22–25, 41
☐ Examples 1-4: Basic: 11–28, 31–35, 38–40, 44–48 Average: 11–41, 44–48 Advanced: 11–48

REACHING ALL LEARNERS – Differentiated Instruction for students with

Developing Knowledge	On-level Knowledge	Advanced Knowledge	English Language Development
☐ Cooperative Learning TE p. 747	☐ Cooperative Learning TE p. 747	☐ Cooperative Learning TE p. 747	☐ Cooperative Learning TE p. 747
☐ Practice A 11-1 CRB	☐ Practice B 11-1 CRB	☐ Practice C 11-1 CRB	☐ Practice A, B, or C 11-1 CRB
☐ Reteach 11-1 CRB		☐ Challenge 11-1 CRB	☐ *Success for ELL* 11-1
☐ Homework Help Online Keyword: MR4 11-1	☐ Homework Help Online Keyword: MR4 11-1	☐ Homework Help Online Keyword: MR4 11-1	☐ Homework Help Online Keyword: MR4 11-1
☐ *Lesson Tutorial Video* 11-1	☐ *Lesson Tutorial Video* 11-1	☐ *Lesson Tutorial Video* 11-1	☐ *Lesson Tutorial Video* 11-1
☐ Reading *Strategies* 11-1 CRB	☐ Problem Solving 11-1 CRB	☐ Problem Solving 11-1 CRB	☐ Reading *Strategies* 11-1 CRB
☐ Questioning Strategies TE p. 747, 749, 750	☐ Multiple Representations TE p. 748	☐ Critical Thinking TE p. 748	☐ Vocabulary Exercises SE p. 746
☐ *IDEA Works!* 11-1			☐ *Multilingual Glossary*

ASSESSMENT
☐ Lesson Quiz, TE p. 754 and Transparency 11-1
☐ State-Specific Test Prep Online Keyword: MR4 TestPrep

Holt Geometry

Lesson Plan 11-2
Arcs and Chords pp. 756–763 Day _____

Objectives Apply properties of arcs. Apply properties of chords.

> **NCTM Standards:** students should analyze characteristics and properties of two-and three-dimensional geometric shapes and develop mathematical arguments about geometric relationships.

Pacing
☐ 45-minute Classes: 1 day   ☐ 90-minute Classes: 1/2 day   ☐ Other_____

WARM UP
☐ Warm Up TE p. 756 and Warm Up Transparency 11-2

TEACH
☐ Lesson Presentation CD-ROM 11-2
☐ Alternate Opener, Exploration Transparency 11-2, TE p. 756
☐ Reaching All Learners TE p. 757
☐ Additional Examples Transparencies 11-2
☐ Teaching Transparency 11-2
☐ *Technology Lab Activities* 11-2
☐ *Know-It Notebook* 11-2

PRACTICE AND APPLY
☐ Examples 1-2: Basic: 19–28, 33, 36 Average: 19–28, 33, 34, 36 Advanced: 19–28, 33, 34, 36, 54
☐ Examples 1-4: Basic: 19–40, 45, 47–50, 55–62 Average: 19–51, 55–62 Advanced: 19–44, 46–62

REACHING ALL LEARNERS – Differentiated Instruction for students with

Developing Knowledge	On-level Knowledge	Advanced Knowledge	English Language Development
☐ Inclusion TE p. 761, 762	☐ Cognitive Strategies TE p. 757	☐ Cognitive Strategies TE p. 757	☐ Cognitive Strategies TE p. 757
☐ Practice A 11-2 CRB	☐ Practice B 11-2 CRB	☐ Practice C 11-2 CRB	☐ Practice A, B, or C 11-2 CRB
☐ Reteach 11-2 CRB		☐ Challenge 11-2 CRB	☐ *Success for ELL* 11-2
☐ Homework Help Online Keyword: MR4 11-2	☐ Homework Help Online Keyword: MR4 11-2	☐ Homework Help Online Keyword: MR4 11-2	☐ Homework Help Online Keyword: MR4 11-2
☐ *Lesson Tutorial Video* 11-2	☐ *Lesson Tutorial Video* 11-2	☐ *Lesson Tutorial Video* 11-2	☐ *Lesson Tutorial Video* 11-2
☐ Reading Strategies 11-2 CRB	☐ Problem Solving 11-2 CRB	☐ Problem Solving 11-2 CRB	☐ Reading Strategies 11-2 CRB
☐ Questioning Strategies TE p. 757, 758, 759	☐ Kinesthetic TE p. 762	☐ Algebra TE p. 757	☐ Vocabulary Exercises SE p. 756
☐ *IDEA Works!* 11-2			☐ *Multilingual Glossary*

ASSESSMENT
☐ Lesson Quiz, TE p. 763 and Transparency 11-2
☐ State-Specific Test Prep Online Keyword: MR4 TestPrep

Holt Geometry

Teacher's Name _____ Class _____ Date _____

Lesson Plan 11-3
Sector Area and Arc Length pp. 764–769   Day _____

Objectives Find the area of sectors. Find arc lengths.

NCTM Standards: students should apply transformations and use symmetry to analyze
  mathematical situations.

Pacing
☐ 45-minute Classes: 1 day   ☐ 90-minute Classes: 1/2 day   ☐ Other_____

WARM UP
☐ Warm Up TE p. 764 and Warm Up Transparency 11-3

TEACH
☐ Lesson Presentation CD-ROM 11-3
☐ Alternate Opener, Exploration Transparency 11-3, TE p. 764
☐ Reaching All Learners TE p. 765
☐ Additional Examples Transparencies 11-3
☐ Teaching Transparency 11-3
☐ *Geometry Lab Activities* 11-3
☐ *Know-It Notebook* 11-3

PRACTICE AND APPLY
☐ Examples 1-2: Basic: 12–15, 26 Average: 12–15, 26, 35 Advanced: 12–15, 26, 35, 37
☐ Examples 1-4: Basic: 12–34, 38–45 Average: 12–35, 38–45 Advanced: 12–45

REACHING ALL LEARNERS – Differentiated Instruction for students with

Developing Knowledge	On-level Knowledge	Advanced Knowledge	English Language Development
☐ Critical Thinking TE p. 765	☐ Critical Thinking TE p. 765	☐ Critical Thinking TE p. 765	☐ Critical Thinking TE p. 765
☐ Practice A 11-3 CRB	☐ Practice B 11-3 CRB	☐ Practice C 11-3 CRB	☐ Practice A, B, or C 11-3 CRB
☐ Reteach 11-3 CRB		☐ Challenge 11-3 CRB	☐ *Success for ELL* 11-3
☐ Homework Help Online Keyword: MR4 11-3	☐ Homework Help Online Keyword: MR4 11-3	☐ Homework Help Online Keyword: MR4 11-3	☐ Homework Help Online Keyword: MR4 11-3
☐ *Lesson Tutorial Video* 11-3	☐ *Lesson Tutorial Video* 11-3	☐ *Lesson Tutorial Video* 11-3	☐ *Lesson Tutorial Video* 11-3
☐ Reading Strategies 11-3 CRB	☐ Problem Solving 11-3 CRB	☐ Problem Solving 11-3 CRB	☐ Reading Strategies 11-3 CRB
☐ Questioning Strategies TE p. 765, 766	☐ Visual TE p. 766, 767	☐ Algebra TE p. 765, 768	☐ Vocabulary Exercises SE p. 764
☐ *IDEA Works!* 11-3			☐ *Multilingual Glossary*

ASSESSMENT
☐ Lesson Quiz, TE p. 769 and Transparency 11-3
☐ State-Specific Test Prep Online Keyword: MR4 TestPrep

Holt Geometry

Lesson Plan 11-4
Inscribed Angles pp. 772–779 Day _____

Objective Find the measure of an inscribed angle. Use inscribed angles and their properties to solve problems.

NCTM Standards: students should compute fluently and make reasonable estimates.

Pacing
☐ 45-minute Classes: 1 day   ☐ 90-minute Classes: 1/2 day ☐ Other_____

WARM UP
☐ Warm Up TE p. 772 and Warm Up Transparency 11-4

TEACH
☐ Lesson Presentation CD-ROM 11-4
☐ Alternate Opener, Exploration Transparency 11-4, TE p. 772
☐ Reaching All Learners TE p. 773
☐ Additional Examples Transparencies 11-4
☐ Teaching Transparency 11-4
☐ *Know-It Notebook* 11-4

PRACTICE AND APPLY
☐ Examples 1-2: Basic: 12–16, 19, 23, 26–32 Average: 12–16, 19, 23, 26–32, 46 Advanced: 12–16, 19, 23, 26–32, 46, 47
☐ Examples 1-4: Basic: 12–30, 33, 35, 36, 39–42, 48–53 Average: 12–44, 48–53 Advanced: 12–53

REACHING ALL LEARNERS – Differentiated Instruction for students with

Developing Knowledge	On-level Knowledge	Advanced Knowledge	English Language Development
☐ Modeling TE p. 773	☐ Modeling TE p. 773	☐ Modeling TE p. 773	☐ Modeling TE p. 773
☐ Practice A 11-4 CRB	☐ Practice B 11-4 CRB	☐ Practice C 11-4 CRB	☐ Practice A, B, or C 11-4 CRB
☐ Reteach 11-4 CRB		☐ Challenge 11-4 CRB	☐ *Success for ELL* 11-4
☐ Homework Help Online Keyword: MR4 11-4	☐ Homework Help Online Keyword: MR4 11-4	☐ Homework Help Online Keyword: MR4 11-4	☐ Homework Help Online Keyword: MR4 11-4
☐ *Lesson Tutorial Video* 11-4	☐ *Lesson Tutorial Video* 11-4	☐ *Lesson Tutorial Video* 11-4	☐ *Lesson Tutorial Video* 11-4
☐ Reading Strategies 11-4 CRB	☐ Problem Solving 11-4 CRB	☐ Problem Solving 11-4 CRB	☐ Reading Strategies 11-4 CRB
☐ Questioning Strategies TE p. 773, 774, 775	☐ Kinesthetic TE p. 773	☐ Critical Thinking TE p. 774, 777	☐ Vocabulary Exercises SE p. 772
☐ *IDEA Works!* 11-4			☐ *Multilingual Glossary*

ASSESSMENT
☐ Lesson Quiz, TE p. 779 and Transparency 11-4
☐ State-Specific Test Prep Online Keyword: MR4 TestPrep

Holt Geometry

Teacher's Name _____ Class _____ Date _____

Lesson Plan 11-5

Angle Relationships in Circles pp. 782–789 Day _____

Objectives Find the measures of angles formed by lines that intersect circles. Use angle measures to solve problems.

| **NCTM Standards:** students should analyze characteristics and properties of two-and three-dimensional geometric shapes and develop mathematical arguments about geometric relationships. |

Pacing
☐ 45-minute Classes: 1 day   ☐ 90-minute Classes: 1/2 day   ☐ Other_____

WARM UP
☐ Warm Up TE p. 782 and Warm Up Transparency 11-5

TEACH
☐ Lesson Presentation CD-ROM 11-5
☐ Alternate Opener, Exploration Transparency 11-5, TE p. 782
☐ Reaching All Learners TE p. 783
☐ Additional Examples Transparencies 11-5
☐ Teaching Transparency 11-5
☐ *Geometry Lab Activities* 11-5
☐ *Know-It Notebook* 11-5

PRACTICE AND APPLY
☐ Examples 1-3: Basic: 16–25, 32, 34–36, 39, 40 Average: 16–25, 32, 34–36, 39, 40, 45 Advanced: 16–25, 32, 34–36, 39, 40, 45, 46
☐ Examples 1-5: Basic: 16–34, 39–44, 49–57 Average: 16–45, 49–57 Advanced: 16–57

REACHING ALL LEARNERS – Differentiated Instruction for students with

Developing Knowledge	On-level Knowledge	Advanced Knowledge	English Language Development
☐ Multiple Representations TE p. 783	☐ Multiple Representations TE p. 783	☐ Multiple Representations TE p. 783	☐ Multiple Representations TE p. 783
☐ Practice A 11-5 CRB	☐ Practice B 11-5 CRB	☐ Practice C 11-5 CRB	☐ Practice A, B, or C 11-5 CRB
☐ Reteach 11-5 CRB		☐ Challenge 11-5 CRB	☐ *Success for ELL* 11-5
☐ Homework Help Online Keyword: MR4 11-5	☐ Homework Help Online Keyword: MR4 11-5	☐ Homework Help Online Keyword: MR4 11-5	☐ Homework Help Online Keyword: MR4 11-5
☐ *Lesson Tutorial Video* 11-5	☐ *Lesson Tutorial Video* 11-5	☐ *Lesson Tutorial Video* 11-5	☐ *Lesson Tutorial Video* 11-5
☐ Reading Strategies 11-5 CRB	☐ Problem Solving 11-5 CRB	☐ Problem Solving 11-5 CRB	☐ Reading Strategies 11-5 CRB
☐ Questioning Strategies TE p. 783, 784, 785	☐ Auditory TE p. 785	☐ Communicating Math TE p. 788	
☐ *IDEA Works!* 11-5			☐ *Multilingual Glossary*

ASSESSMENT
☐ Lesson Quiz, TE p. 789 and Transparency 11-5
☐ State-Specific Test Prep Online Keyword: MR4 TestPrep

73

Holt Geometry

Lesson Plan 11-6
Segment Relationships in Circles pp. 792–798   Day _____

Objectives Find the lengths of segments formed by lines that intersect circles. Use the lengths of segments in circles to solve problems.

NCTM Standards: students should analyze characteristics and properties of two-and three-dimensional geometric shapes and develop mathematical arguments about geometric relationships.

Pacing
☐ 45-minute Classes: 1 day   ☐ 90-minute Classes: 1/2 day   ☐ Other_____

WARM UP
☐ Warm Up TE p. 792 and Warm Up Transparency 11-6

TEACH
☐ Lesson Presentation CD-ROM 11-6
☐ Alternate Opener, Exploration Transparency 11-6, TE p. 792
☐ Reaching All Learners TE p. 793
☐ Additional Examples Transparencies 11-6
☐ Teaching Transparency 11-6
☐ *Geometry Lab Activities* 11-6
☐ *Know-It Notebook* 11-6

PRACTICE AND APPLY
☐ Examples 1-2: Basic: 12–15, 22, 23 Average: 12–15, 22, 23, 28 Advanced: 12–15, 22, 23, 28, 38
☐ Examples 1-4: Basic: 12–28, 32, 35, 40–47 Average: 12–36, 40–47 Advanced: 12–26, 28–47

REACHING ALL LEARNERS – Differentiated Instruction for students with

Developing Knowledge	On-level Knowledge	Advanced Knowledge	English Language Development
☐ Visual Cues TE p. 793	☐ Visual Cues TE p. 793	☐ Visual Cues TE p. 793	☐ Visual Cues TE p. 793
☐ Practice A 11-6 CRB	☐ Practice B 11-6 CRB	☐ Practice C 11-6 CRB	☐ Practice A, B, or C 11-6 CRB
☐ Reteach 11-6 CRB		☐ Challenge 11-6 CRB	☐ *Success for ELL* 11-6
☐ Homework Help Online Keyword: MR4 11-6	☐ Homework Help Online Keyword: MR4 11-6	☐ Homework Help Online Keyword: MR4 11-6	☐ Homework Help Online Keyword: MR4 11-6
☐ *Lesson Tutorial Video* 11-6	☐ *Lesson Tutorial Video* 11-6	☐ *Lesson Tutorial Video* 11-6	☐ *Lesson Tutorial Video* 11-6
☐ Reading Strategies 11-6 CRB	☐ Problem Solving 11-6 CRB	☐ Problem Solving 11-6 CRB	☐ Reading Strategies 11-6 CRB
☐ Questioning Strategies TE p. 793, 794	☐ Algebra TE p. 796	☐ Science Link TE p. 797	☐ Vocabulary Exercises SE p. 792
☐ *IDEA Works!* 11-6			☐ *Multilingual Glossary*

ASSESSMENT
☐ Lesson Quiz, TE p. 798 and Transparency 11-6
☐ State-Specific Test Prep Online Keyword: MR4 TestPrep

Holt Geometry

Lesson Plan 11-7

Circles in the Coordinate Plane pp. 799–805   Day _____

Objectives Write equations and graph circles in the coordinate plane. Use the equation and graph of a circle to solve problems.

NCTM Standards: students should apply appropriate techniques, tools, and formulas to determine measurements.

Pacing
☐ 45-minute Classes: 1 day   ☐ 90-minute Classes: 1/2 day   ☐ Other_____

WARM UP
☐ Warm Up TE p. 799 and Warm Up Transparency 11-7

TEACH
☐ Lesson Presentation CD-ROM 11-7
☐ Alternate Opener, Exploration Transparency 11-7, TE p. 799
☐ Reaching All Learners TE p. 800
☐ Additional Examples Transparencies 11-7
☐ Teaching Transparency 11-7
☐ *Know-It Notebook* 11-7

PRACTICE AND APPLY
☐ Examples 1-3: Basic: 10–35, 37–40, 42–44, 48–54 Average: 10–45, 48–54 Advanced: 10–54

REACHING ALL LEARNERS – Differentiated Instruction for students with

Developing Knowledge	On-level Knowledge	Advanced Knowledge	English Language Development
☐ Multiple Representations TE p. 800	☐ Multiple Representations TE p. 800	☐ Multiple Representations TE p. 800	☐ Multiple Representations TE p. 800
☐ Practice A 11-7 CRB	☐ Practice B 11-7 CRB	☐ Practice C 11-7 CRB	☐ Practice A, B, or C 11-7 CRB
☐ Reteach 11-7 CRB		☐ Challenge 11-7 CRB	☐ *Success for ELL* 11-7
☐ Homework Help Online Keyword: MR4 11-7	☐ Homework Help Online Keyword: MR4 11-7	☐ Homework Help Online Keyword: MR4 11-7	☐ Homework Help Online Keyword: MR4 11-7
☐ *Lesson Tutorial Video* 11-7	☐ *Lesson Tutorial Video* 11-7	☐ *Lesson Tutorial Video* 11-7	☐ *Lesson Tutorial Video* 11-7
☐ Reading Strategies 11-7 CRB	☐ Problem Solving 11-7 CRB	☐ Problem Solving 11-7 CRB	☐ Reading Strategies 11-7 CRB
☐ Questioning Strategies TE p. 800, 801	☐ Critical Thinking TE p. 803	☐ Technology TE p. 800	
☐ *IDEA Works!* 11-7			☐ *Multilingual Glossary*

ASSESSMENT
☐ Lesson Quiz, TE p. 805 and Transparency 11-7
☐ State-Specific Test Prep Online Keyword: MR4 TestPrep

Holt Geometry

Lesson Plan 12-1
Reflections pp. 824–830 Day _____

Objective Identify and draw reflections.

NCTM Standards: students should analyze change in various contexts.

Pacing
☐ 45-minute Classes: 1 day ☐ 90-minute Classes: 1/2 day ☐ Other_____

WARM UP
☐ Warm Up TE p. 824 and Warm Up Transparency 12-1

TEACH
☐ Lesson Presentation CD-ROM 12-1
☐ Alternate Opener, Exploration Transparency 12-1, TE p. 824
☐ Reaching All Learners TE p. 825
☐ Additional Examples Transparencies 12-1
☐ Teaching Transparency 12-1
☐ *Geometry Lab Activities* 12-1
☐ *Know-It Notebook* 12-1

PRACTICE AND APPLY
☐ Examples 1-2: Basic: 13–18, 24–26, 28–30 Average: 13–18, 24–26, 28–30, 43–45, 52 Advanced: 13–18, 24–26, 28–30, 43–45, 52–57
☐ Examples 1-4: Basic: 13–37, 40, 41, 46–48, 58–66 Average: 13–23, 24–36 even, 37–51, 58–66 Advanced: 13–23, 24–36 even, 37–66

REACHING ALL LEARNERS – Differentiated Instruction for students with

Developing Knowledge	On-level Knowledge	Advanced Knowledge	English Language Development
☐ Auditory Cues TE p. 825	☐ Auditory Cues TE p. 825	☐ Auditory Cues TE p. 825	☐ Auditory Cues TE p. 825
☐ Practice A 12-1 CRB	☐ Practice B 12-1 CRB	☐ Practice C 12-1 CRB	☐ Practice A, B, or C 12-1 CRB
☐ Reteach 12-1 CRB		☐ Challenge 12-1 CRB	☐ *Success for ELL* 12-1
☐ Homework Help Online Keyword: MR4 12-1	☐ Homework Help Online Keyword: MR4 12-1	☐ Homework Help Online Keyword: MR4 12-1	☐ Homework Help Online Keyword: MR4 12-1
☐ *Lesson Tutorial Video* 12-1	☐ *Lesson Tutorial Video* 12-1	☐ *Lesson Tutorial Video* 12-1	☐ *Lesson Tutorial Video* 12-1
☐ Reading *Strategies* 12-1 CRB	☐ Problem Solving 12-1 CRB	☐ Problem Solving 12-1 CRB	☐ Reading *Strategies* 12-1 CRB
☐ Questioning Strategies TE p. 825, 826	☐ Science TE p. 828	☐ Technology TE p. 826	☐ Vocabulary Exercises SE p. 824
☐ *IDEA Works!* 12-1			☐ *Multilingual Glossary*

ASSESSMENT
☐ Lesson Quiz, TE p. 830 and Transparency 12-1
☐ State-Specific Test Prep Online Keyword: MR4 TestPrep

Holt Geometry

Lesson Plan 12-2

Translations pp. 831–837   *Day* _____

Objective Identify and draw translations.

> **NCTM Standards:** students should analyze change in various contexts.

Pacing
☐ 45-minute Classes: 1 day   ☐ 90-minute Classes: 1/2 day   ☐ Other_____

WARM UP
☐ Warm Up TE p. 831 and Warm Up Transparency 12-2

TEACH
☐ Lesson Presentation CD-ROM 12-2
☐ Alternate Opener, Exploration Transparency 12-2, TE p. 831
☐ Reaching All Learners TE p. 832
☐ Additional Examples Transparencies 12-2
☐ Teaching Transparency 12-2
☐ *Know-It Notebook* 12-2

PRACTICE AND APPLY
☐ Examples 1-2: Basic: 12–17, 24, 25 Average: 12–17, 25, 26, 36–38, 44 Advanced: 12–17, 25, 26, 36–38, 44–49
☐ Examples 1-4: Basic: 12–27, 29–35, 40–42, 50–57 Average: 12–43, 50–57 Advanced: 12–57

REACHING ALL LEARNERS – Differentiated Instruction for students with

Developing Knowledge	On-level Knowledge	Advanced Knowledge	English Language Development
☐ Home Connection TE p. 832	☐ Home Connection TE p. 832	☐ Home Connection TE p. 832	☐ Home Connection TE p. 832
☐ Practice A 12-2 CRB	☐ Practice B 12-2 CRB	☐ Practice C 12-2 CRB	☐ Practice A, B, or C 12-2 CRB
☐ Reteach 12-2 CRB		☐ Challenge 12-2 CRB	☐ *Success for ELL* 12-2
☐ Homework Help Online Keyword: MR4 12-2	☐ Homework Help Online Keyword: MR4 12-2	☐ Homework Help Online Keyword: MR4 12-2	☐ Homework Help Online Keyword: MR4 12-2
☐ *Lesson Tutorial Video* 12-2	☐ *Lesson Tutorial Video* 12-2	☐ *Lesson Tutorial Video* 12-2	☐ *Lesson Tutorial Video* 12-2
☐ Reading Strategies 12-2 CRB	☐ Problem Solving 12-2 CRB	☐ Problem Solving 12-2 CRB	☐ Reading Strategies 12-2 CRB
☐ Questioning Strategies TE p. 832, 833	☐ Technology TE p. 832	☐ Probability TE p. 835	
☐ *IDEA Works!* 12-2			☐ *Multilingual Glossary*

ASSESSMENT
☐ Lesson Quiz, TE p. 837 and Transparency 12-2
☐ State-Specific Test Prep Online Keyword: MR4 TestPrep

Holt Geometry

Lesson Plan 12-3
Rotations pp. 839–845   Day _____

Objective Identify and draw rotations.

NCTM Standards: students should use visualization, spatial reasoning, and geometric modeling to solve problems.

Pacing
☐ 45-minute Classes: 1 day   ☐ 90-minute Classes: 1/2 day   ☐ Other_____

WARM UP
☐ Warm Up TE p. 839 and Warm Up Transparency 12-3

TEACH
☐ Lesson Presentation CD-ROM 12-3
☐ Alternate Opener, Exploration Transparency 12-3, TE p. 839
☐ Reaching All Learners TE p. 840
☐ Additional Examples Transparencies 12-3
☐ Teaching Transparency 12-3
☐ *Know-It Notebook* 12-3

PRACTICE AND APPLY
☐ Examples 1-2: Basic: 13–18, 24–30, 32–34 Average: 13–18, 24–30, 32–34 Advanced: 13–18, 24–30, 32–34, 42, 46
☐ Examples 1-4: Basic: 13–31, 41, 42–44, 52–59 Average: 13–31, 35, 37–46, 52–59 Advanced: 13–31, 35, 37–59

REACHING ALL LEARNERS – Differentiated Instruction for students with

Developing Knowledge	On-level Knowledge	Advanced Knowledge	English Language Development
☐ Inclusion TE p. 840	☐ Concrete Manipulatives TE p. 840	☐ Concrete Manipulatives TE p. 840	☐ Concrete Manipulatives TE p. 840
☐ Practice A 12-3 CRB	☐ Practice B 12-3 CRB	☐ Practice C 12-3 CRB	☐ Practice A, B, or C 12-3 CRB
☐ Reteach 12-3 CRB		☐ Challenge 12-3 CRB	☐ *Success for ELL* 12-3
☐ Homework Help Online Keyword: MR4 12-3	☐ Homework Help Online Keyword: MR4 12-3	☐ Homework Help Online Keyword: MR4 12-3	☐ Homework Help Online Keyword: MR4 12-3
☐ *Lesson Tutorial Video* 12-3	☐ *Lesson Tutorial Video* 12-3	☐ *Lesson Tutorial Video* 12-3	☐ *Lesson Tutorial Video* 12-3
☐ Reading Strategies 12-3 CRB	☐ Problem Solving 12-3 CRB	☐ Problem Solving 12-3 CRB	☐ Reading Strategies 12-3 CRB
☐ Questioning Strategies TE p. 840, 841	☐ Visual TE p. 842, 844	☐ Technology TE p. 841	
☐ *IDEA Works!* 12-3			☐ *Multilingual Glossary*

ASSESSMENT
☐ Lesson Quiz, TE p. 845 and Transparency 12-3
☐ State-Specific Test Prep Online Keyword: MR4 TestPrep

Holt Geometry

Lesson Plan 12-4
Compositions of Transformations pp. 848–853   Day _____

Objectives Apply theorems about isometries. Identify and draw compositions of transformations, such as
  glide reflections.

NCTM Standards: students should analyze characteristics and properties of two-and three-
  dimensional geometric shapes and develop mathematical arguments about geometric relationships.

Pacing
☐ 45-minute Classes: 1 day   ☐ 90-minute Classes: 1/2 day   ☐ Other_____

WARM UP
☐ Warm Up TE p. 848 and Warm Up Transparency 12-4

TEACH
☐ Lesson Presentation CD-ROM 12-4
☐ Alternate Opener, Exploration Transparency 12-4, TE p. 848
☐ Reaching All Learners TE p. 849
☐ Additional Examples Transparencies 12-4
☐ Teaching Transparency 12-4
☐ *Know-It Notebook* 12-4

PRACTICE AND APPLY
☐ Examples 1-3: Basic: 8–19, 22–25, 29–36 Average: 8–25, 29–36 Advanced: 8–13, 15–36

REACHING ALL LEARNERS – Differentiated Instruction for students with

Developing Knowledge	On-level Knowledge	Advanced Knowledge	English Language Development
☐ Modeling TE p. 848	☐ Modeling TE p. 848	☐ Modeling TE p. 848	☐ Modeling TE p. 848
☐ Practice A 12-4 CRB	☐ Practice B 12-4 CRB	☐ Practice C 12-4 CRB	☐ Practice A, B, or C 12-4 CRB
☐ Reteach 12-4 CRB		☐ Challenge 12-4 CRB	☐ *Success for ELL* 12-4
☐ Homework Help Online Keyword: MR4 12-4	☐ Homework Help Online Keyword: MR4 12-4	☐ Homework Help Online Keyword: MR4 12-4	☐ Homework Help Online Keyword: MR4 12-4
☐ *Lesson Tutorial Video* 12-4	☐ *Lesson Tutorial Video* 12-4	☐ *Lesson Tutorial Video* 12-4	☐ *Lesson Tutorial Video* 12-4
☐ Reading Strategies 12-4 CRB	☐ Problem Solving 12-4 CRB	☐ Problem Solving 12-4 CRB	☐ Reading Strategies 12-4 CRB
☐ Questioning Strategies TE p. 848, 849	☐ Reading Math TE p. 848	☐ Kinesthetic TE p. 850, 852	☐ Vocabulary Exercises SE p. 848
☐ *IDEA Works!* 12-4			☐ *Multilingual Glossary*

ASSESSMENT
☐ Lesson Quiz, TE p. 853 and Transparency 12-4
☐ State-Specific Test Prep Online Keyword: MR4 TestPrep

Holt Geometry

Teacher's Name _____ Class _____ Date _____

Lesson Plan 12-5
Symmetry pp. 856–862 Day _____

Objective Identify and describe symmetry in geometric figures.

> **NCTM Standards:** students should analyze characteristics and properties of two-and three-dimensional geometric shapes and develop mathematical arguments about geometric relationships.

Pacing
☐ 45-minute Classes: 1 day   ☐ 90-minute Classes: 1/2 day ☐ Other_____

WARM UP
☐ Warm Up TE p. 856 and Warm Up Transparency 12-5

TEACH
☐ Lesson Presentation CD-ROM 12-5
☐ Alternate Opener, Exploration Transparency 12-5, TE p. 856
☐ Reaching All Learners TE p. 857
☐ Additional Examples Transparencies 12-5
☐ Teaching Transparency 12-5
☐ *Know-It Notebook* 12-5

PRACTICE AND APPLY
☐ Examples 1-2: Basic: 13–18, 23–32, 34–36, 38–42, 47–49 Average: 13–18, 23–32, 34–36, 38–42, 47–49, 55 Advanced: 13–18, 23–32, 34–36, 38–42, 47–49, 55–59
☐ Examples 1-4: Basic: 13–43, 45, 47–49, 51–54, 63–69 Average: 13–28, 30–55, 63–69 Advanced: 13–28, 30–36 even, 37–69

REACHING ALL LEARNERS – Differentiated Instruction for students with

Developing Knowledge	On-level Knowledge	Advanced Knowledge	English Language Development
☐ Modeling TE p. 857	☐ Modeling TE p. 857	☐ Modeling TE p. 857	☐ Modeling TE p. 857
☐ Practice A 12-5 CRB	☐ Practice B 12-5 CRB	☐ Practice C 12-5 CRB	☐ Practice A, B, or C 12-5 CRB
☐ Reteach 12-5 CRB		☐ Challenge 12-5 CRB	☐ *Success for ELL* 12-5
☐ Homework Help Online Keyword: MR4 12-5	☐ Homework Help Online Keyword: MR4 12-5	☐ Homework Help Online Keyword: MR4 12-5	☐ Homework Help Online Keyword: MR4 12-5
☐ *Lesson Tutorial Video* 12-5	☐ *Lesson Tutorial Video* 12-5	☐ *Lesson Tutorial Video* 12-5	☐ *Lesson Tutorial Video* 12-5
☐ Reading Strategies 12-5 CRB	☐ Problem Solving 12-5 CRB	☐ Problem Solving 12-5 CRB	☐ Reading Strategies 12-5 CRB
☐ Questioning Strategies TE p. 857, 858	☐ Visual TE p. 859	☐ Critical Thinking TE p. 862	☐ Vocabulary Exercises SE p. 856
☐ *IDEA Works!* 12-5			☐ *Multilingual Glossary*

ASSESSMENT
☐ Lesson Quiz, TE p. 862 and Transparency 12-5
☐ State-Specific Test Prep Online Keyword: MR4 TestPrep

Holt Geometry

Lesson Plan 12-6
Tessellations pp. 863–869   Day _____

Objectives Use transformations to draw tessellations. Identify regular and semiregular tessellations and figures that will tessellate.

NCTM Standards: students should analyze characteristics and properties of two-and three-dimensional geometric shapes and develop mathematical arguments about geometric relationships.

Pacing
☐ 45-minute Classes: 1 day   ☐ 90-minute Classes: 1/2 day   ☐ Other_____

WARM UP
☐ Warm Up TE p. 863 and Warm Up Transparency 12-6

TEACH
☐ Lesson Presentation CD-ROM 12-6
☐ Alternate Opener, Exploration Transparency 12-6, TE p. 863
☐ Additional Examples Transparencies 12-6
☐ Teaching Transparency 12-6
☐ *Technology Lab Activities* 12-61
☐ Teaching Transparency 12-6
☐ *Know-It Notebook* 12-6

PRACTICE AND APPLY
☐ Examples 1-2: Basic: 15–20, 28–33, 37–41 Average: 15–20, 28–33, 37–41, 43, 44 Advanced: 15–20, 28–33, 37–41, 43, 44, 49
☐ Examples 1-4: Basic: 15–41, 43, 44, 46–48, 53–60 Average: 15–50, 53–60 Advanced: 15–60

REACHING ALL LEARNERS – Differentiated Instruction for students with

Developing Knowledge	On-level Knowledge	Advanced Knowledge	English Language Development
☐ Multiple Representations TE p. 864	☐ Multiple Representations TE p. 864	☐ Multiple Representations TE p. 864	☐ Multiple Representations TE p. 864
☐ Practice A 12-6 CRB	☐ Practice B 12-6 CRB	☐ Practice C 12-6 CRB	☐ Practice A, B, or C 12-6 CRB
☐ Reteach 12-6 CRB		☐ Challenge 12-6 CRB	☐ *Success for ELL* 12-6
☐ Homework Help Online Keyword: MR4 12-6	☐ Homework Help Online Keyword: MR4 12-6	☐ Homework Help Online Keyword: MR4 12-6	☐ Homework Help Online Keyword: MR4 12-6
☐ *Lesson Tutorial Video* 12-6	☐ *Lesson Tutorial Video* 12-6	☐ *Lesson Tutorial Video* 12-6	☐ *Lesson Tutorial Video* 12-6
☐ Reading Strategies 12-6 CRB	☐ Problem Solving 12-6 CRB	☐ Problem Solving 12-6 CRB	☐ Reading Strategies 12-6 CRB
☐ Questioning Strategies TE p. 864, 865	☐ Kinesthetic TE p. 864, 867	☐ Science Link TE p. 868	☐ Vocabulary Exercises SE p. 863
☐ *IDEA Works!* 12-6			☐ *Multilingual Glossary*

ASSESSMENT
☐ Lesson Quiz, TE p. 869 and Transparency 12-6
☐ State-Specific Test Prep Online Keyword: MR4 TestPrep

Holt Geometry

Lesson Plan 12-7
Dilations pp. 872–879   Day _____

Objective Identify and draw dilations.

NCTM Standards: students should analyze characteristics and properties of two-and three-dimensional geometric shapes and develop mathematical arguments about geometric relationships.

Pacing
☐ 45-minute Classes: 1 day   ☐ 90-minute Classes: 1/2 day   ☐ Other_____

WARM UP
☐ Warm Up TE p. 872 and Warm Up Transparency 12-7

TEACH
☐ Lesson Presentation CD-ROM 12-7
☐ Alternate Opener, Exploration Transparency 12-7, TE p. 872
☐ Reaching All Learners TE p. 873
☐ Additional Examples Transparencies 12-7
☐ Teaching Transparency 12-7
☐ *Know-It Notebook* 12-7

PRACTICE AND APPLY
☐ Examples 1-2: Basic: 13–18, 24–29, 33 Average: 13–18, 24–29, 42–45 Advanced: 13–18, 24–29, 33, 42–45
☐ Examples 1-4: Basic: 13–41, 46–49, 52–56 Average: 13–49, 51–56 Advanced: 13–30, 32–56

REACHING ALL LEARNERS – Differentiated Instruction for students with

Developing Knowledge	On-level Knowledge	Advanced Knowledge	English Language Development
☐ Inclusion TE p. 875	☐ Critical Thinking TE p. 873	☐ Critical Thinking TE p. 873	☐ Critical Thinking TE p. 873
☐ Practice A 12-7 CRB	☐ Practice B 12-7 CRB	☐ Practice C 12-7 CRB	☐ Practice A, B, or C 12-7 CRB
☐ Reteach 12-7 CRB		☐ Challenge 12-7 CRB	☐ *Success for ELL* 12-7
☐ Homework Help Online Keyword: MR4 12-7	☐ Homework Help Online Keyword: MR4 12-7	☐ Homework Help Online Keyword: MR4 12-7	☐ Homework Help Online Keyword: MR4 12-7
☐ *Lesson Tutorial Video* 12-7	☐ *Lesson Tutorial Video* 12-7	☐ *Lesson Tutorial Video* 12-7	☐ *Lesson Tutorial Video* 12-7
☐ Reading Strategies 12-7 CRB	☐ Problem Solving 12-7 CRB	☐ Problem Solving 12-7 CRB	☐ Reading Strategies 12-7 CRB
☐ Questioning Strategies TE p. 873, 874	☐ Algebra TE p. 874	☐ Algebra TE p. 874	☐ Vocabulary Exercises SE p. 872
☐ *IDEA Works!* 12-7			☐ *Multilingual Glossary*

ASSESSMENT
☐ Lesson Quiz, TE p. 879 and Transparency 12-7
☐ State-Specific Test Prep Online Keyword: MR4 TestPrep

Holt Geometry